BARON · DOCTOR FAUSTUS

HUMANISTISCHE BIBLIOTHEK

ABHANDLUNGEN · TEXTE · SKRIPTEN

In Verbindung mit dem 'Centro Italiano di Studi Umanistici e Filosofici' und dem 'Center for Medieval and Renaissance Studies of Barnard College', Columbia University, sowie dem 'Institute for Vico Studies', N.Y.

Herausgegeben von Ernesto Grassi
Redaktion Eckhard Keßler

REIHE I: ABHANDLUNGEN

BAND 27

FRANK BARON

DOCTOR FAUSTUS
FROM HISTORY TO LEGEND

1978

WILHELM FINK VERLAG MÜNCHEN

For James Sloan

ISBN 3-7705-1539-0

© 1978 Wilhelm Fink Verlag, München
Satz und Druck: Brönner & Daentler KG, Eichstätt
Bindung: Graph. Betrieb Schöningh, Paderborn

Gedruckt mit Unterstützung der Alexander von Humboldt-Stiftung

TABLE OF CONTENTS

Introduction	7
I. Who was Faustus?	11
II. At the University of Heidelberg	17
III. Faustus and his Contemporaries:	
Johannes Trithemius	23
Mutianus Rufus	39
The Bishop of Bamberg	42
Kilian Leib	45
Joachim Camerarius	48
IV. The Death of Faustus	67
V. Luther and the New Image of Faustus	70
VI. The Metamorphosis of Faustus	83
Notes	89
Index	112

INTRODUCTION

> Mein Freund, die Zeiten der Vergangenheit
> Sind uns ein Buch mit sieben Siegeln.
> Was ihr den Geist der Zeiten heißt,
> Das ist im Grund der Herren eigner Geist,
> in dem die Zeiten sich bespiegeln.
>
> Goethe, *Faust*

Recent studies have failed to present a comprehensive and convincing biography of the man who was the catalyst for one of the most important legends of modern times. A quotation from a relatively new book on the Faust tradition reflects the confusing aspect of this situation: "There is no coherent biography of the historical Faust. The image that we have of him is a colorful mosaic, patched together from incidental and sharply contradictory statements of contemporaries – and often even in these cases legend and reality are closely intertwined."[1] A bibliography lists 183 articles and books containing information about the historical Doctor Faustus.[2] Arranged in chronological order, these scholarly works reflect a marked progress in the accumulation of significant biographical data. But it is a fact that inconsistencies still plague the image of the historical Faustus.

The blame for this perplexing situation lies not with the nature of the accumulated biographical information but rather with the lack of critical studies distinguishing between reliable and misleading evidence about the historical Faustus. A stricter application of common-sense rules of admissible evidence, the consideration of the motives of contemporaries writing about Faustus, and the rejection of source materials hitherto assumed to be reliable clear the way for an understanding of the entire process from history to legend.

This kind of analysis, while focusing on evidence about a unique historical personality, demonstrates the manner in which certain powerful historical forces operated in the sixteenth century to transform the image of Faustus and make it a vivid symbol of significant concerns and beliefs at that time.

The legend of Faustus developed in two distinct stages. The first, the historical stage, indicates his contemporaries' reaction to the personality of the historical Faustus. This Faustus was closely linked to ideas about the occult; the nature of the reactions to Faustus and his occult interests or practices shows a very important phenomenon of the age in which he lived and which gave birth to his legend: the renaissance of the occult sciences in the academic world. An awareness of the assumptions behind the contemporary reactions makes the personality of Faustus emerge in a consistent fashion. Since even the very first reactions to Faustus imply significant deviations from historical truth, one is justified in maintaining that the legend was born within Faustus' lifetime.

The second stage of the legend shows far more radical distortions of historical facts. Indeed, it appears that this second stage, influenced primarily by the views of Martin Luther, represents the negative reactions not only to a single individual, now perceived primarily through hearsay, but also to a wide range of assumptions that shaped the earliest image of Faustus. The development in this second stage, culminating in the publication of the chapbook *(Volksbuch)* of 1587, went beyond simply rejecting the personality of Faustus; it evolved into a polemic, which condemned certain premises on which the society of the pre-Reformation era made its judgments. The problem of Faustus and the origin of the Faustus legend becomes thus a problem of understanding the significant social, political, and religious forces that initiated the literature about this famous figure. The anonymous Protestant author of the 1587 chapbook claimed to be writing a genuine historical work about Faustus, but in fact he was simply compiling and organizing anecdotes, the interpretation of which was prepared by men like Luther and Melanchthon.

A similar legend about Faustus might have been written by a Catholic author. After all, the persecution of witches, which became very intense in the middle of the sixteenth century (when the clear outlines of the Faustus legend first became perceptible), was not a monopoly of the Protestants.[3] But it was the fate of the Faustus legend to be drawn gradually into the orbit of the polemical Luther and other Reformation writers. Here the audacity and boldness of Faustus the magician, representing an age with a much more liberal attitude toward the occult, was punished by a fictional linking with the devil and subsequent condemnation to an eternal life in hell.

My interpretation of the early evolution of the legend is not compatible with the inclination of previous scholarship to grant credibility to most early sources. Hans Henning's recent biographical study of Faustus represents the most comprehensive consideration of these materials. In spite of its apparent thoroughness, Henning's interpretation fails to detect basic changes in the evolution of Faustus up to 1587. Henning mistakenly assumes the reliability of pronouncements about Faustus by Melanchthon, as well as by other authors writing as late as about twenty-five years after the probable time of Faustus' death.[4] Yet even the earliest primary sources reflect a strong subjective element. Discussions of the occult in the sixteenth century appear to have had a strong tendency to invite polemics and to generate embellishments and exaggerations.

The old adage "When Peter talks about Paul, you learn more about Peter than about Paul" is certainly applicable to the source materials relating to Faustus. Similarly, the Faust of Goethe's drama argues that men who seek to discover the spirit of former ages – like Faust's famulus Wagner – succeed in uncovering not objective reality but the reflection of their own ideas. Strongly subjective elements dominate the reports, anecdotes, and even scholarly works about Faustus. This study attempts to reconstruct the motivations and forces operating to transform, cover up, and destroy knowledge about objective history. A clear distinction between objective, factual statements, on the one hand, and subjective, speculative elements, on the other, is essential; only the former relate to the historical Faustus, while the latter relate primarily to the development of the legend. This distinction makes it possible to observe the imprint of at least two historical eras, the Renaissance and the Reformation. One might visualize a historical process in analogy to the phenomenon of geological stratification. From this perspective the legendary Faustus of the Reformation appears to have been superimposed on the historical Faustus of the Renaissance. This kind of view would not be a novelty in historical research: Heinrich Schliemann, looking for Homer's Troy, was confronted, in a very concrete sense, by the problem of stratification and the need to make clear distinctions between the stages leading from fact to legend.[5] Fortunately, evidence about the activities of Faustus, in contrast to other figures who have inspired legends, has been preserved in reliable reports, making the consistent and coherent reconstruction of his historical and legendary life possible.

While engaged in research as a postdoctoral fellow of the Alexander von Humboldt-Stiftung in Munich, I became aware of the deficiencies in previous scholarship on the historical Faustus. I am grateful to the Humboldt-Stiftung and to the University of Kansas (General Research Fund) for financial support.

For help, encouragement, and constructive criticism I owe gratitude most of all to my wife, Betty, as well as to Professors Bernhard Bischoff, Frank Borchardt, Hans Eggers, Ernesto Grassi, William S. Heckscher, C. Stephen Jaeger, Ludwig Krapf, Eckhard Kessler, and James Sloan.

I

WHO WAS FAUSTUS?

> *Georgius Faustus Helmstetensis*
> Kilian Leib, 1528
>
> *Novi quendam nomine (Iohannem) Faustus de Kundling* ...
> Melanchthon/Manlius, 1562
>
> *Doctor Faustus ist eines Bauwern Sohn gwest, zu Rod, bey Weimar bürtig*...
> Historia von D. Iohann Fausten, 1587

There are many Fausts. Most of them are products of the modern literary imagination, far removed from the legendary Faust of the sixteenth century, and even farther from the original historical character. Faust has become a symbol for modern ideas and ideals, and each new Faust figure has reflected primarily the weltanschauung or beliefs of its creator. Thus, the progressive stages of the Faust tradition correspond to significant developments in modern intellectual history. But there can be no doubt that a single Faustus (as he was called in the sixteenth century) served as the original catalyst in the development of the entire Faust tradition.

One of the fundamental problems relating to the beginnings of the Faust tradition is that scholars have not been able to arrive at a consensus about the elementary question: what was the name of the historical Faustus? One eminent German scholar, Will-Erich Peuckert, has gone so far as to suggest that there must have been at least two Fausts, Johann and Georg, a father and son, both of whom were involved in the practice of occult sciences.[1] This view has not been accepted, but neither has there been a serious attempt to explain how two presumably reliable sources could use different first names to refer to the same person. Thus, the strange existence of both names side by side is assumed as a fact in a recent study by Hans Henning and in the article "Faust" in the new German biographical dictionary.[2]

Our study will try to show that the cause of this confusion lies in a faulty evaluation of the available evidence. The name Johann (or Johannes) does not appear at all in the earliest sources. It is linked to the name Faustus for the first time in 1562, about twenty-five years after the probable time of the man's death. The legend had by this time erased the memory of the historical Faustus. The credibility of this late source as historical evidence must be questioned very seriously, even if the faith it has inspired in so many scholars ever since its publication may appear understandable. The author responsible for causing the confusion about the name of Faustus was Johannes Manlius, a student at the University of Wittenberg. He edited a work entitled *Locorum communium collectanea*, a very popular book of anecdotes and aphorisms based on the lectures of his eminent teacher Philipp Melanchthon.[3]

The anecdotes are enlivened by polemics against Faustus. They focus on the devil's role behind Faustus' magical feats and violent death. The fact that these anecdotes were based on the testimony of a highly respected figure of the Reformation has caused scholars to overlook their tone of fantasy and hearsay. Yet it is doubtful that Melanchthon – who, like Luther, was extremely superstitious in matters relating to the occult – gave any reliable information about Faustus.[4] Moreover, the editor Johannes Manlius did not handle the original material from his teacher very scrupulously; he changed it and added to it to make his presentation more interesting reading. Having such a tenuous background, the name Johannes, which subsequently replaced the Georg of the earlier sources, has significance primarily for understanding the development of a legend of Faustus. This topic will be treated in detail later. (Cf. chapter V)

Since it does not appear in any reliable contemporary source, the name Johann must be rejected as the name of the historical figure.

The willingness to dispense with Manlius' report makes a basically consistent reconstruction of Faustus' life possible. But before turning to the details of such a reconstruction, we must examine the reliability of the primary sources. What is unique about these sources is that they are direct products of a confrontation with Faustus and that the context of this confrontation and the circumstances that led to the recording of specific information can be reconstructed. It is precisely these qualities that Manlius' report lacks.

Whereas many possibilities for the distortion of information about Faustus are conceivable in the case of Manlius' report, they are considerably reduced in the case of the information found in eight available contemporary documents: three individual official notations in city and diocese records, an entry in a diary, and letters of four different contemporaries who had encountered Faustus personally. The listing below gives the dates and authors of the source materials together with the names ascribed to Faustus:

August 20, 1507	–	Johannes Trithemius: "Magister Georgius Sabellicus Faustus iunior"[5]
October 3, 1513	–	Conrad Mutianus Rufus: "Georgius Faustus Helmitheus Hedelbergensis"[6]
February 12, 1520	–	Hans Müller: "Doctor Faustus philosoph(us)"[7]
June 17, 1528	–	An Ingolstadt scribe: "Doctor Jörg Faustus von Haidlberg"[8]
July, 1528	–	Kilian Leib: "Georgius Faustus Helmstet(ensis)"[9]
May 10, 1532	–	Hieronymus Holzschuher: "Doctor Faust(us)"[10]
August 13, 1536	–	Joachim Camerarius: "Faustus"[11]
January 15, 1540	–	Philipp von Hutten: "Philosophus Faustus"[12]

We have not considered a number of interesting and possibly illuminating sources that originated after 1540 because there is no way to reestablish the original context of the source materials. Since these sources were written down after the legend of Faustus was widespread, there is no way to be sure that the information provided was not in some way influenced by it. This does not mean that these sources are totally unreliable. But it is no longer certain what part can be entirely credible.[13] The most widely circulated printed sources will be discussed in the chapter concerned with the origin of the legend.

On the basis of these sources it is possible to make reliable generalizations about the name, birthplace, and studies of Faustus. In this consideration the precise form of Faustus' name is of decisive significance. It is evident that the name associated with the historical figure in question was Faustus rather than Faust. In the sixteenth century people were aware of the basic difference between the Latin word *faustus* (fortunate or auspicious) and the German word *Faust* (fist), which is often found as a family name. Since then this distinction has been overlooked; the inclination among biographers of Faustus (especially since the time of Lessing and Goethe) to think of "Faust" rather than "Faustus" has been the source of a number of misunderstandings.

For example, one scholar tried to identify Faustus as an alumnus of Heidelberg, and he located a certain Johannes Faust von Symmern in the university records. But this student began his studies in December 1505 and received his bachelor's degree in 1509, long after Faustus had claimed a master's degree. Recently, Hans Henning has argued persuasively against the relevance of this Johannes Faust to the historical figure, but because of his adherence to the name Faust rather than Faustus, the next step in his argument appears suspect. Henning writes that the rejection of the hypothesis about Johannes Faust von Symmern forces him to the conclusion that "Faust's" claim to an academic title must be considered fraudulent. According to Henning, no German university matriculation records contain any entry that would apply to "Faust."[14] Of course, if he had assumed the actual Latin name of Faustus as his point of departure, Henning might have arrived at a different result.

If it is assumed that "Faustus" was the correct name, it may be further inferred that the person involved replaced his original German family name, in the manner of most humanists at this time, with an assumed Latin name. The use of the name "Faustus" thus becomes a significant piece of biographical information, indicating that its bearer attached special importance to the form of his name and consequently made the deliberate decision to rename himself in an individual and novel way. This implication is confirmed in the earliest available source, where the name Faustus follows "Sabellicus." Like "Faustus", this name is of Latin origin and cannot by any stretch of the imagination be interpreted as a German name. The use of "sabellicus" as a name indicates that the bearer wished to be identified as one who came from an area north of Rome, the land of the Sabines, particularly famous for the practice of the occult from the time of Roman antiquity up to the sixteenth century.[15] The choice of both uncommon names implies an attempt to advertise a certain degree of academic sophistication and, at the same time, a desire to appear mysterious. The Latin word *faustus* was, of course, particularly apt for one whose chief occupation was to predict future events, just as "sabellicus," implying an ancestry going back to the magicians of antiquity, was appropriate for one who claimed to be a *magus*. By the choice of symbolic names Faustus was the deliberate author of his reputation, not unlike Luther, who renamed himself with a Greek word in Latinized form, Eleutherius (= liberator), just when he became aware of his historical role as a reformer, in the period 1516-9.[16] There are, of course, countless examples of Latin and Greek names among the humanists of the Renaissance.

A study of the names used in the sixteenth century to refer to Faust indicates that the form "Faust" first appeared in 1565, in a German translation of Manlius' *Collectanea*, but even after that the form "Faustus" predominated. Lessing and Goethe, who did not make use of the sixteenth-century sources, used the form "Faust," and their overwhelming influence tended to erase the memory of the original Latin name. While Faustus' name is not particularly significant for the treatment of literary questions, it is an elementary and decisive one in the search for the historical figure.

The primary sources do not reveal Faustus' family name. This peculiarity is worth noting and will be of interest later. On the other hand, the sources are consistent in their references to the first name Georgius or its German equivalent, Georg or Jörg. The name Johannes does not appear in any of these early sources; it is again only after the numerous printings on Manlius' report that this name becomes widespread, finally being adopted in the chapbook of 1587. The original name Georgius was associated with Faustus in a number of less well-known anecdotes, even as late as 1592.[17]

Although the names Georgius and Faustus are consistent in the primary sources, at first glance the place names appear inconsistent. Sources cite two different places: Heidelberg and Helmstadt. In fact, there is no contradiction; both names could have referred to the same geographic area, Heidelberg in a more general sense and Helmstadt, a village near Heidelberg, in a very precise sense. It was common practice for a person who came from a small town to identify himself with the large city in the vicinity. A famous example of this custom is Nicolaus von Cues (Cusanus), who in Italy, where people could not be expected to recognize Cues, called himself Nicolaus Treverensis (i.e., of Trier). Conrad Celtis also illustrates this point. He registered at the University of Heidelberg as Conrad Celtis from Würzburg. Later, when he took his master's examination he cited the more precise designation of his home town: Wyttfeld, a small village near Würzburg.[18] It may be assumed, then, that Georgius Faustus was born in Helmstadt, but for the sake of simplicity often referred to his birthplace as Heidelberg instead of the little village of Helmstadt. Therefore, the most likely explanation for the otherwise baffling name of Helmitheus in Mutianus Rufus' letter about Faustus is that it is a corrupted form of Helmstadius or Helmstetius. Since the hand that wrote "Helmitheus" also wrote "Hedelbergensis" instead of "Heidelbergensis," such a spelling error would not appear unusual.[19] At any rate, the primary sources indicate clearly that the place where the historical Faustus was born was not Kundling or Knittlingen, as it was asserted in later sources, but rather Helmstadt near Heidelberg.

Another apparent inconsistency lies in the different academic titles associated with Faustus: *magister, doctor,* and *philosophus*. As in the case of the Heidelberg-Helmstadt problem, the question of the differences here can be resolved by a clarification of a practice in the sixteenth century. At that time the acquisition of the title *magister* entailed the study of philosophy, specifically Aristotelian philosophy according to the scholastic method, about one to two years beyond the bachelor's degree. The master's degree was the highest degree possible in philosophy. In general, the title *doctor* was reserved for those who had obtained the highest degree in theology, law, or medicine, but not uncommonly the master of arts in philosophy was also called *doctor*.[20] In this light, Faustus' claim to an academic title appears consistent and precise, indicating extensive university training.

It is reasonable to assume that a young man who lived in Helmstadt would choose Heidelberg rather than another place for his university studies. One might expect to find the name of Faustus in the university records, but research into them has not yielded any references to a person with this particular name. The search for a Georgius from Helmstadt, however, has brought positive results.[21] A student by this name did indeed study there from 1483 until 1487, when he received his master's degree in philosophy. Although the name Faustus is not linked anywhere in the records with the name Georgius Helmstetter, there are certain indications that this Heidelberg student was the same Faustus referred to in the primary sources. Like Faustus, the student was reluctant to reveal his family name. The records show his name in a number of variations (Georgius Helmstetter, Jorio de Helmstat, Jeorius de Helmstat, Georio de Helmstadt, Jeorius Helmstadt) but each case is conspicuous for its incompleteness.[22] Students of that time usually indicated their surnames, and during the semester in which Helmstetter registered at Heidelberg only one other student from a total of sixty-seven elected not to do so. Thus the young Helmstetter demonstrated the same reluctance to reveal his surname that Faustus later consistently displayed.

Very few young men from small villages like Helmstadt ever had the chance to attend the university. During the years 1460 to 1520 a total of thirteen students came from Helmstadt, four graduating with bachelor's degrees and only two obtaining master's degrees. There is no trace of another Georgius Helmstetter at this time. Under these circumstances it is unlikely that the exact correspondence of name and scope of academic training is simply a coincidence. Moreover, the kind of education the Heidelberg graduate of 1487 had received manifests itself in a number of ways in the subsequent activities of the historical Doctor Faustus.

II

AT THE UNIVERSITY OF HEIDELBERG

> *Nur so viel läßt ... sich schließen, daß er einen gewissen Grad geistiger Kultur und humanistischer Bildung erlangt hat, was ihm auf autodidaktischem Wege kaum möglich gewesen wäre.*
> Georg Witkowski, "Der historische Faust" (1897)

Georg Helmstetter of the Worms Diocese registered at the University of Heidelberg on January 9, 1483.[1] After a period of only one and a half years Helmstetter applied to take his bachelor's examination. His application was considered at a meeting of the examination commission of the Faculty of Arts. The candidate lacked a number of the requirements, including one relating to the length of study *(defectus temporis)*.[2] The statutes required at least a year and a half of study for this degree. If one counts from the date of registration to the actual date of his graduation on July 12, 1484, Helmstetter appears to have met this requirement, though just barely. But because of his arrival in the middle of the academic year and because he came so close to the minimum time allowed, he was probably unable to attend all the required courses. Magister Johannes Hasse vouched for the fact that Helmstetter would make up within a reasonable period of time whatever was still expected of him. A few days later Helmstetter was able to graduate, and then for three years he continued his studies towards a master's degree.[3] Before he could be granted the advanced degree his case had to be considered again by an examination commission because of requirements not completed. Helmstetter had taken part in only two of the three formal disputations required, and he was enjoined to participate in yet another one before his examination. Then on March 1, 1487, he graduated as a *magister*, ranking second among ten candidates. To preside at his graduation ceremony Helmstetter chose Magister Syrus Lubler, who had also presided at the awarding of his bachelor's degree. Soon afterwards, on March 20, the newly graduated master was administered the oath required for use of the Faculty of Arts library. The notation about this is the last indication about his activities at the University of Heidelberg. But he still needed to fulfill his obligation to teach two years in the Faculty of Arts, for the statutes required this of all newly graduated masters. Hence Helmstetter probably remained in Heidelberg at least through the summer semester of 1489.[4]

The most striking aspect of Helmstetter's academic training at Heidelberg was the speed with which he obtained his bachelor's degree. At this time the average length of study in Heidelberg was two years. In contrast, the span of three years (1484-1487) for the master's degree appears relatively long. Many masters obtained this degree within a year; the average time was about 1.75 years. This oddity may be due to the fact that Helmstetter absented himself from his studies for a time. On the other hand, for an apparently ambitious student like Helmstetter the slowdown in his rate of progress may have occurred simply because of his youthful age. The minimum age allowed a student to obtain his master's degree in Germany at this time was either twenty or twenty-one years.[5] The statutes of Ingolstadt and Greifswald prescribed twenty-years of age, and although the Heidelberg statutes do not refer to this matter, some requirement undoubtedly existed. Helmstetter's pattern of studies is very similar to that of the humanist Hartmann Schedel, who, having registered at Leipzig in 1456, obtained his bachelor's degree one year later, after which time he spent three years in pursuit of a master's degree before graduating in 1460 at the age of twenty.[6] The case of Rudolf Agricola was similar: he registered at Erfurt in 1456 when he was only twelve years old. He is said to have received his bachelor's degree two years later. Although he continued his studies at Köln and Louvain, he did not receive his master's degree from the University of Louvain until 1465 when he was twenty-one years old.[7] This common phenomenon suggests that, as he approached his master's examination, Helmstetter, too, was shy of the minimum age of twenty or twenty-one. Accordingly, the probable date of his birth was 1466 or 1467.[8]

Although Georg Helmstetter showed a tendency to do only the minimum work required for his degrees, his graduation as a *magister* near the top of his class demonstrates that he had the intellectual ability to cope with the intricacies of logic and philosophy. Like his fellow students, he had spent many hours of intensive study trying to understand Aristotle, and he had trained himself in the art of scholastic disputations.

Since 1452, students at Heidelberg enjoyed the freedom of choice between two opposing methods of interpreting Aristotle: between the *via moderna* and the *via antiqua*. The former looked primarily to the authority of William of Ockham and maintained the nominalistic position, that universals were only class names; whereas the latter, the *via antiqua*, with Thomas Aquinas as its main authority, generally held the belief that the universals had existence.[9] The *via moderna*, which Helmstetter joined, had been the sole school of thought permitted before the reformers of the *via antiqua* succeeded in gaining recognition. But the *via moderna* remained the larger philosophic camp, continuing to graduate the majority of students. Neither side offered a significant deviation from the traditional scholastic curriculum. Perhaps the *via moderna*, with its insistence on extensive use of commentaries as developed by Marsilius von Inghen, the founder of the university, could be said to have been the more conservative group of students and faculty.

After scholastic philosophy, the strongest single influence a student like Helmstetter was exposed to in Heidelberg at the time was Renaissance humanism or, to use the term that was current at that time, the *studia humanitatis*. During the last two decades of the fifteenth century the University of Heidelberg became famous in Germany as a center of humanistic studies. Through the efforts of Peter Luder, Stephan Hoest, and Jacob Wimpfeling in the preceding three decades the *studia humanitatis* had become an important factor in university life at Heidelberg. Although humanistic studies still were not part of the traditional course of scholastic requirements, their influence was felt in every area of academic activity. During the 1480s some of the most famous German humanists were living in Heidelberg: Rudolph Agricola, Conrad Celtis, Johannes von Dalberg, Dietrich von Pleningen, Johannes Reuchlin, and Johannes Trithemius.

In 1480, having returned from his studies in Italy, Johannes von Dalberg was named provost (Domprobst) in Worms and this office carried with it the title of Chancellor of the University of Heidelberg. Two years later, he became Bishop of Worms and Chancellor of the Elector of the Palatinate. Another humanist, Dietrich von Pleningen, was an advisor to the Elector Philipp, making Heidelberg extremely attractive to humanists in search of patrons.

Rudolph Agricola came to Heidelberg in 1484. Agricola, Dalberg and Pleningen had studied together in Ferrara, and they were among the first representatives of Greek studies in Germany.[10] The university records are silent about their humanistic activities, but according to later reports, Agricola took an active part in the life of the university, holding lectures on Pliny the Younger with some regularity, and attending scholastic disputations. He was long remembered in Heidelberg for the wide scope of his knowledge in philosophy and for his acute critical abilities.[11] Drawn by the fame of Dalberg and Agricola, Conrad Celtis, who had obtained his bachelor's degree in Köln, registered in Heidelberg on December 10, 1484. He obtained his master's degree on October 20, 1485. Thus, although Celtis belonged to the *via antiqua,* his advanced philosophical studies overlapped for a time with those of Helmstetter.

The primary interests of Celtis lay, of course, not in scholastic philosophy but in poetry and rhetoric, which he combined with elementary studies in Greek and Hebrew. A number of sources indicate that men like Celtis, Agricola, Dalberg, and Trithemius became interested in Hebrew studies at this time, and they employed private tutors to teach them the rudiments of the language in Heidelberg. The most famous German Hebrew scholar was Johannes Reuchlin, who was closely associated with this humanistic circle. According to him, Dalberg's library contained an extremely rich collection of Latin, Greek, and Hebrew books. Reuchlin dedicated the earliest fruits of his studies to Dalberg: *Colloquia graeca* (1489) a collection of Greek conversations with Latin translations, and *De verbo mirifico* (1494), a dialogue that treats the relevance of Jewish mysticism (i.e., cabala) to Christian thought. According to one report, Dalberg himself composed a treatise on the secret mysteries of numbers *(De numerorum arcanis mysteriis).*[12]

It is evident that the entire humanistic school at Heidelberg was very much under the influence of the neoplatonic and hermetic writings of Ficino and Pico in Florence. The revival of Hermes Trismegistus made magic respectable in the scholarly world, although Renaissance thinkers were careful to define their area of interest as "natural magic," in contrast to the prohibited black magic. The scholarly interest in natural magic gave a strong impetus to the flourishing of all occult sciences. Hence, at the University of Heidelberg, where the interest in astrology and magic was never totally absent, students had the opportunity to learn a great deal about the occult.

A student who attained the highest degree in philosophy at a German university in the fifteenth century had at least a cursory exposure to the area that was generally called mathematics, but which actually entailed a combination of astronomy and astrology. For the master's degree the Heidelberg statutes prescribed two astronomical works that had been used in universities since the thirteenth century; *De sphaera* by Johannes de Sacrobosco and the *Theorica Planetarum* by Gerhard of Cremona.[13] In the higher ranks of the *via moderna* the study of astronomy was considered particularly valuable to the fame of the faculty and the university. This fact comes to light in the rules of the *Collegium Dionysium,* an association of masters in the field of theology, which promoted this field of study with particular vigor, although it was found necessary to warn against the prohibited arts.[14] In his autobiographical notes a certain Conrad Buitzius states that in his bachelor's examination he questioned the legality of believing in, practicing, and studying the arts of magic. The same autobiographical notes show that Buitzius spent some time copying information about astronomy, necromancy, and geomancy.[15] Jodocus Eichmann, one of the founders of the *via antiqua* in Heidelberg, studied the occult sciences; he wrote (or copied?) a tract on chiromancy.[16] Numerous surviving manuscripts from the old university library in Heidelberg indicate that the interest in astrology was particularly strong. Many tracts of Arabic astrologers were copied, and the prognostications for particular years were recorded.[17]

The precise nature of the influence that these humanistic activities and the academic interest in the occult had on Helmstetter is a matter of conjecture. University students generally had little direct contact with the humanists like Dalberg and Pleningen, who spent more time at the court of the elector than in the lecture halls. Nonetheless, this court was within walking distance of the university, and the students could not fail to notice how greatly the intellectual achievements of these men were respected at the courts as well as at the universities throughout Germany. Moreover, if Helmstetter became interested at this time in astrology and magic, he must have sensed that these mysterious subjects were acquiring a new image of respectability as well as popularity. The age during which Faustus lived and became famous experienced a great renaissance of the ancient occult sciences. In the sixteenth century the rulers, the scholarly world, and the general populace were all influenced by the promises of astrologers and magicians. The beginnings of this significant development were already taking shape at Heidelberg in the 1480s.

An awareness of Faustus' studies in Heidelberg helps to shed light on the motivations behind his later pronouncements and activities. Having become a wandering astrologer and magician, he did not have the kind of career that one might expect with his extensive education. But what we know from reliable sources does not allow us to doubt seriously that he had indeed studied at Heidelberg. We have already noted his tendency to advertise himself as magister, doctor and philosopher. By adopting a Latin name he showed the desire to have the appearance of humanistic learning. In fact, reports about his boasting as a magician reflect a considerable humanistic bias; at the same time, he was willing to risk debate on the foremost authority of the scholastics, Aristotle. It is evident that Faustus was proud of his academic background and that this background enhanced his prestige as an astrologer and magician. He could claim, after all, to be more than the common magician. Although he was attacked, there were respectable people from the academic world who marvelled at him and did not question his competence as a philosopher. If other philosophers like Trithemius and Camerarius criticized him, one must take into account that these critics were themselves competitors in the area of the occult. In its proper context the metamorphosis of Faustus from his academic beginnings to an unorthodox wandering "scholar" appears consistent and plausible.

III

FAUSTUS AND HIS CONTEMPORARIES: *Johannes Trithemius*

> *Magiam autem naturalem, quam Picus Mirandola, neque damnatam ab Ecclesia unquam fuisse, neque posse damnari scribit, multi Ecclesiastici viri doctissimi approbaverunt, & secuti sunt.*
>
> *Haec est magia mea, quam sequor: alteram vero, quae superstitiosa, diabolica, & ab Ecclesia sancta jure damnata, nulli fidelium est licita, execro, abhorreo, despicio penitus, cum suis authoribus condemno.*
>
> Trithemius, *Nepiachus*

Johannes Trithemius' letter of August 20, 1507, to Johannes Virdung von Haßfurt supplies the earliest evidence about the activities of Doctor Faustus and represents the most comprehensive biographical facts about Faustus' life. But it is a polemical letter, intended to discredit Faustus. Trithemius saw himself as a philosopher and rejected Faustus' claims to genuine knowledge in this field. Taken at face value, the words of Trithemius tend to show an extremely interesting but one-sided image. To distinguish historical facts from possible distortions, it is essential to investigate the background of this letter – the eccentric ideas and strange motives that shaped Trithemius' attitude toward Faustus. His statements about Faustus reflect his own personality and interests to a considerable extent, and this must be taken into account in order to arrive at a correct interpretation of the letter.

Trithemius was a paradoxical figure. An abbot, he was also a bibliographer, historian, and advisor to German princes. At the Benedictine monastery of Sponheim, where he served as abbot for twenty-three years, he built up one of the most impressive collections of manuscripts and books of his time. He had close ties to the foremost humanists of Germany. He displayed a wide range of religious and humanistic interests, which are reflected in a rich correspondence and in numerous published works. The most unique aspect of his many interests was the one that touched on the interests of Faustus; Trithemius' zealous dedication to the occult was truly unusual. This interest, to be sure, was related to a strong mystical tendency in his religious thought. For Trithemius, natural magic was the key to the perception of divine nature, which he called the "One," as well as to the achievement of miraculous feats.

It was not uncommon for Trithemius to have intense religious experiences, such as visions and sudden revelations.[1] In his letter to Arnold Bostius, dated March 25, 1499, Trithemius described a momentous revelation he had experienced in his study of occult matters. This letter is important in helping to show what Trithemius saw as the essence of his work as a philosopher. It is important, moreover, because the general circulation of this letter had serious consequences for his reputation.

Trithemius writes to Bostius that he is in the process of writing a great work entitled *Steganographia,* which, in his opinion, is destined to amaze the world. He explains that the first four books deal with methods of secret writing, communicating thoughts without written words, with or without a messenger, to faraway persons so that the message cannot be discovered by anyone except the person for whom it was intended, teaching someone to read or write Latin in a matter of a couple of hours, and experiments in communicating ideas without words or signs to persons otherwise fully occupied. But then Trithemius goes on in the fifth book to speak of the amazing fruits of his work, which he does not intend to make public. In order to counteract rumors that might have reached Bostius' ears, he insists that he is not a magician but a philosopher.[2] Trithemius compares himself to Albert the Great who had risked being thought a magician by the common populace. Trithemius emphasizes that what he knows came to him by way of a revelation. One night someone appeared to him at his bedside and taught him in his sleep all that he had vainly sought for many days.[3] Trithemius intended to write down what he had thus learned, but no one except one prince was to see his work, for he feared that his secrets might be misused for evil ends. The letter closed without any precise indication of what the great revelation had been.

It is not surprising that these strange occupations of the anything but modest abbot became the source of difficulties. The letter never reached its intended recipient. Bostius had died before its arrival, and it was opened and circulated by unfriendly hands, to become the source of hostile rumors.

For the rest of his life Trithemius suffered from the burden of a reputation as a magician. In many subsequent writings he attempted to disprove the claims made against him and to restore his good name.[4]

The elaborate plan for the *Steganographia* described to Bostius was never completely realized. During his lifetime Trithemius completed only two books and part of a third. The fragment was published posthumously in 1606. Like its companion volume *Polygraphia*, published in 1508, the surviving fragments of the *Steganographia* reflect primarily an interest in cryptography. Trithemius scholars have treated these works in some detail.[5] But the works reflect only a limited aspect of Trithemius' occult studies. If we search for the momentous revelations Trithemius had intimated in his letter to Bostius, we will be disappointed. To discover what insights had inspired the great excitement of these revelations, we must turn to certain other letters.

Two letters of 1503, one to Count Johannes von Westerburg and the other to Elector Joachim von Brandenburg, show great affinity to the revelations made to Bostius.[6] They explain in some detail the intricacies and implications of "natural magic." As in his letter to Bostius, Trithemius confides his secrets reluctantly, stressing that they are not to be given to the ignorant masses. He repeats his earlier fear that his secrets in the wrong hands could become the cause of evil. Again he indicates the usefulness of his wisdom for princes. Even the style of these letters, reflecting the great excitement of a momentous discovery, is very much reminiscent of the revelations made to Bostius.

For Trithemius the key to natural magic lay in numerology. He expounded on its essential principles most explicitly in a letter to Germanus de Ganay. This exposition of natural magic, written on August 24, 1505, provides a significant background for the encounter with Faustus. It is particularly important because Trithemius related his position on natural magic to other occult sciences, and his severe criticism of alchemy and astrology is closely related to his condemnation of Faustus, in whom he recognized a representative of the deceitful practice of the same occult sciences.

Trithemius writes to Ganay: "The Three *(ternarius)* must be led back entirely to Unity *(unitas)* if the mind is to attain perfect knowledge of these phenomena. For the One *(unarius)* is not a number; every number arises from it. The Two *(binarium)* must be rejected, and it is possible to convert the Three back to Unity. This is the truth, Germanus, as Hermes says, certain without falsity and absolutely true through the knowledge of Unity."[7]

This numerological operation was for Trithemius the fundamental principle that made natural magic possible. The emphasis on the One as the key to perfect knowledge is reminiscent of the Pythagorean school, which viewed the One as the power that held the world together.[8] But by quoting Hermes at this point Trithemius identified the sources of his wisdom also with Hermes Trismegistus and the latter's Renaissance interpreters.

Ficino's translation (first published in 1471) of the writings attributed to Hermes Trismegistus was a significant catalyst in the development of the Renaissance conception of natural magic. Ficino saw Hermes as one of the earliest and greatest sources of wisdom, from whom there was a direct link to Plato's philosophy. He considered Hermes as a prophet who foresaw the coming of Christ, as well as an ancient practitioner and teacher of philosophical magic, which was not forbidden by the Church. Under the influence of Hermetic writings Ficino popularized the concept of natural magic, which embraced a very wide scope of scientific, philosophical, and religious ideas, but which claimed not to resort to the aid of evil spirits. Although the Renaissance theorists of natural magic were generally learned humanists, they continued to make use of many magical concepts and practices of the Middle Ages (e.g., incantations, talismans, astrological terminology, etc.).

Giovanni Pico della Mirandola was deeply impressed by the Hermetic writings, and under Ficino's influence he became an enthusiastic proponent of natural magic. In 1486 Pico offered to defend nine hundred theses, a considerable number of which were devoted to magic. A significant innovation of theses was the demonstration of the great affinity that existed between natural magic and cabala. There was no science, according to Pico, that made us more certain of the divinity of Christ than magic and cabala. Although this thesis was later condemned by a papal commission, Pico's arguments in defense of this particular conclusion made an impression on contemporaries and found a strong echo in Germany.[9]

Trithemius was an avid reader of Pico's works, which were represented by many volumes in his library.[10] From Pico, Trithemius might have learned that numbers made the profound secrets of nature accessible.[11] Like Trithemius, Pico had found it necessary to attack other contemporary occult practices, especially astrology, and Pico was the most famous proponent of the conviction that natural magic should be practiced only by a select few and should not be popularized for the masses.[12]

Trithemius referred also to Johannes Reuchlin as his teacher.[13] Reuchlin's writings, especially his notions about cabala, undoubtedly influenced Trithemius, but the most important source of the particular kind of natural magic

Trithemius favored was a Frenchman named Libanius Gallus, who visited Trithemius at Sponheim in 1495. Libanius professed to be a Platonist and a pupil of Pico.[14] The correspondence between Trithemius and Libanius suggests that the numerology fundamental to Trithemius' natural magic developed out of the encounter with Libanius. Trithemius revered Libanius as a trustworthy mentor and received from him "great and miraculous philosophical secrets" as well as advice about propitious occult practices. Libanius encouraged his pupil to become a Pythagorean.[15] Libanius was well acquainted with the numerological principle of "returning the Three to the One," which Trithemius had tried to explain in letters as early as 1503, for in a letter of 1507 Trithemius confided to Libanius that he was still occupied with this problem.[16]

For Trithemius the speculations about numbers represented an attempt to escape the limitations of the physical realm. This explains in part his attitude to other occult sciences. In his letter to Germanus, Trithemius stressed that his magic was purely spiritual, not dependent on any phenomena in the physical world:

> ... the alchemists make promises with reference to compound bodies, but they err; they are deceived, and they deceive everyone who willingly listens to them. They want to imitate nature and to divide what is exclusively whole, since they do not understand the basis of virtue and nature ... Our philosophy is not earthly but rather celestial so that we might perceive that highest principle, which we call God ... Let unadvised men depart, idle men, the lying astrologers, deceivers, frivolous babblers. For the disposition of the stars does not contriubte anything to the immortal mind, nothing to natural science, and nothing to supercelestial wisdom. Substance has no control over anything except substance. The mind is free; it is not subject to the stars; it is not susceptible to their influences; it does not follow motion, but rather a supercelestial principle by which it was created and by which it communicates so much.[17]

Thus, for Trithemius natural magic entailed solely operations of the mind. The traditional alchemists and astrologers, in contrast, derived their wisdom from the study of the physical world. Trithemius did not quarrel with the aims of the alchemists and astrologers, only with their methods. His own approach made use of spiritual concepts exclusively: "Study generates cognition; cognition gives birth to love; love to similitude; similitude to communion; communion to virtue; virtue to dignity; dignity to power, and power produces miracle. This is the sole path to the perfect magic, divine as well as natural..."[18]

A strong current of religious fervor underlies these speculations. Trithemius contemplated the ascent to magical power and miracle just as the mystics contemplated the ascent to the union with God.[19] There is no reason to doubt the sincerity of Trithemius' religious feelings. The source and practical results of his thought relate, however, primarily to the Hermetic tradition, on the outer perimeter of orthodox religion.[20]

In 1506 Trithemius resigned from his postition as abbot of Sponheim to become abbot of the monastery of Saint James, just outside Würzburg. The circumstances surrounding this unusual change were very painful and humiliating for Trithemius. His close ties to Elector Philipp of the Palatinate had undoubtedly made enemies for him, because this prince was thought to be responsible for the wars that ravaged the vicinity of Sponheim in 1504 and 1505. The monks turned against Trithemius, who, rather than attempting to bring about a reconciliation, abandoned the monastery where he had served as an abbot for twenty-three years and where he had built up his famous library.[21]

The Bibliotheca Vaticana has a manuscript of the letters Trithemius wrote during this period. The entire manuscript was addressed to his step-brother Jacob, to whom the work of emendation and eventual publication was entrusted. The letters of this collection reflect the great emotional crisis Trithemius had endured on account of the numerous attacks on his reputation. He hoped that the letters would restore his good name. From these letters it is clear that his damaged reputation resulted not only from his political affiliations and the hostility of his monks but also from the rumors circulating about him as a magician. In his letter of August 16, 1507, to Johannes Cappelarius, Trithemius expressed his concern about these rumors: "... I have accomplished nothing stupendous, and yet I have to contend with the opinion of the masses, many thinking that I am a magus; they claim seriously that I have raised the dead, brought up demons from the underworld, foretold the future, and captured thieves with incantations."[22]

Trithemius made these remarks in a letter he grouped together with his defense of natural magic to Germanus de Ganay and his attack on Faustus to Johannes Virdung. Thus, the position taken against Faustus must be seen in the context of an attempt to defend a damaged reputation as well as to justify his particular kind of occult interests. The letter about Faustus gave Trithemius an opportunity to attack occult practices he considered deceptive and even sinful, thus making his own philosophic position on magic appear more justifiable.

> ... That man, about whom you wrote me, Georgius Sabellicus, who dared to call himself the foremost of the necromancers, is an unstable character, a babbler, and a vagabond. He deserves to be thrashed in order to prevent him from heedlessly and continuously asserting in public things that are abominable and contrary to the teachings of the Holy Church. What are his assumed titles if not the manifestations of an extremely muddled mind, showing him to be a fool rather than a philosopher? For he composed a calling card to suit his taste: Magister Georgius Sabellicus, Faustus junior, the inspiration of necromancers, astrologer, the secund magus, palmist, practitioner of divination with the use of high places and fire, and second in the art of divination with the use of water. Behold the foolishness of this man; with what great madness does he dare to call himself the inspiration of necromancers. One who is ignorant of all good arts should call himself a jester rather than a master of the arts. But I am not blind to his wickedness. When I returned from the Mark Brandenburg last year, I came upon this man in the town of Gelnhausen. In the inn I received reports of the many worthless things he had promised with great rashness. As soon as he heard that I was present, he fled from the inn, and he could not be persuaded by any means to come and meet me. The same foolish calling card he gave to you, and which I mentioned, he also sent to me by means of someone in town. Certain priests in the town reported to me that in the presence of many people he claimed to have acquired such comprehensive wisdom and memory that if all the works of Plato and Aristotle with the whole body of their philosophical thought completely disappeared from the memory of man, he himself, through his genius, like another Ezra, could restore all things with a greater degree of elegance. Later, while I stayed in Speyer, he traveled to Würzburg, and, driven by the same foolishness, he is reported to have said in the presence of many people that the miracles of Christ were not so amazing; he himself could do all the things Christ had done, as often as and whenever one desired. Towards the end of Lent this year he came to Kreuznach, and, boasting with similar folly, he promised even more remarkable things, contending that in alchemy he surpassed all previous masters and that he understood and could accomplish whatever people wished. In the meantime, a teaching position became vacant in Kreuznach and he was appointed to it on the recommendation of Franz von Sickingen, an

official of your prince and a man very fond of the occult. With the most criminal kind of design he soon began to seduce the boys, and when this behavior was suddenly brought to light, he eluded certain punishment by fleeing. These things are known to me through the most reliable evidence about the man whose arrival you await with such ardent desire. When he comes to you, you will find that he is not a philosopher but rather a very rash fool. Greetings. Remember me to the Prince if the opportunity arises. From Würzburg on the twentieth day of August in the year of our Lord 1507.

Johannes Virdung von Haßfurt, an astrologer to whom Trithemius wrote about Faustus, was no less interested in occult matters. Since 1493 he had been in the service of the Elector of the Palatinate in Heidelberg. He had studied at the Universities of Cracow and Leipzig. Manuscripts at the Bibliotheca Vaticana preserve astronomical as well as astrological texts written by his hand. Here one finds evidence of a strong interest in magic. Virdung wrote down information about imprisoning the planets in rings, and he copied magical images ascribed to Hermes. In 1503 the traveled to England for the express purpose of studying magic.[23] Virdung was the author of numerous astrological works; he was accustomed to publishing annual predictions. Philipp Melanchthon was an admirer of Virdung's astrological skills and consulted him in matters relating to his future.[24]

The letter of Trithemius shows that Virdung was anxiously awaiting a meeting with Faustus ("...quem tanto esse desiderio prestolaris."),[25] and that he had written to Trithemius earlier ("Homo ille de quo mihi scripsisti..."), probably seeking information about this prospective visitor. Furthermore, Virdung had been the recipient of the same calling card that Faustus had sent to Trithemius ("Titulum stultitae suae qualem dedit ad te quem memoravimus, per quendam civem ad me quoque destinavit."). The information that both Trithemius and Virdung had received the same calling card from Faustus is important because it makes it very likely that Trithemius reported the content of the card accurately. Being aware that Virdung had the same information, Trithemius must have been all the more careful not to harm his own credibility by inaccuracy. This calling card, therefore, represents a reliable piece of evidence, conveying Faustus' own words. It is unique because no other document has survived from which the written or spoken words of Faustus could be reliably adduced. Trithemius himself also reported on certain claims Faustus had made, but he made these reports on the basis of second-hand information, and they are, therefore, less reliable.

An awareness of Virdung's interest in magic and his eagerness to meet Faustus tends to counterbalance the onesidedly negative image presented by Trithemius. The calling card, which for Trithemius reflected a charlatan's work, elicited in Virdung eager interest and expectation. On closer inspection, Faustus' calling card does leave room for various interpretations, making the two widely divergent reactions plausible.

Trithemius never actually came face to face with Faustus. Returning from his lengthy visit from the Elector Joachim of Brandenburg in Berlin, he was forced to remain in Leipzig for six days on account of a kidney stone. Then he continued on to Gotha, where he met his friend Conrad Mutianus Rufus briefly. He finally arrived in Gelnhausen, a town between Fulda and Frankfurt, toward the end of May, 1506.[26] At the inn where he was staying, Trithemius received a report of statements Faustus had made, and he was apparently interested in talking to him. "As soon as he (Faustus) heard that I was present, he fled from the inn, and he could not be persuaded by any means to come to meet me. The same foolish calling card he gave to you, and which I mentioned, he also sent to me by means of someone in town." The following information was on the card that Trithemius received from Faustus:

> Magister Sabellicus, Faustus iunior, fons necromanticorum, astrologus, magus secundus, chiromanticus, agromanticus, pyromanticus, in hydra arte secundus.

The occult sciences in which Faustus claimed expertise were not unlike those found in the context of discussions of magic and divination in many literary works of the Middle Ages. As *astrologus* and *magus* Faustus associated himself with famous professions that were well known to every period of history. But as a practitioner of *necromantia* (divination through communication with the dead), *chiromantia* (palm reading), *pyromantia* (divination from fire), and *hydromantia* (divination from water), Faustus revealed his closeness to a popular tradition of the Middle Ages. In the *Ackermann aus Böhmen* (chapter 26), written about a hundred years before, these occult sciences are grouped together with other arts and sciences that men use to acquire knowledge. Only one form of divination listed by Faustus, *agromanticus*, is difficult to account for as an occupation known in the Middle Ages, and it has been a source of puzzlement among scholars.[27] Since the word *agromanticus* was listed immediately before references to divination by fire and water, one might expect a word here indicating divination by one of the other two elements, air or earth, i.e., *aeromanticus* or *geomanticus*. But in his autobiographical essay *Nepiachus* (1508), written about the same time as the letter about Faustus, Trithemius uses the word *acromantia* (= *agromantia*) next to *eromantia* (= *aeromantia*) and *geomantia*, implying that agromantia was a distinct occult practice.²⁸ Moreover, John Tenchard in his *Natural History of Superstition* (1709) refers to acromancy as one of the forms of divination. Thus, there is no reason to suppose that there is a mistake in the original text. The possible relationship to the Greek word ἄκρος (= at the end, extreme, at the top; as in Acropolis) suggests a form of divination having to do with high places.²⁹

Another unique element is that Faustus referred to himself as the "second" magus and the "second" in the divination from water. He was willing to concede, consequently, in these two areas at least (in necromancy and alchemy Faustus claimed to be first!), that there were those who were superior to him. Who were they? According to a long literary tradition in the Middle Ages, going back to the authority of Isidor and Augustine, the first magus was Zoroaster.³⁰ Similarly, the first famous practitioner of hydromancy was the Roman king Numa Pompilius, from the land of the Sabines. This, too, had become a popular idea in the literature of the Middle Ages, again largely on the authority of Augustine.³¹ Thus, under the guise of modesty, by recognizing superiors, Faustus was actually boasting about his learning, showing that he was aware of the literary tradition relating to magic and divination.

This kind of boasting is also evident in the names Faustus adopted. As noted in chapter I, the name Sabellicus indicates that the bearer "came" from the land of the Sabines. Thus, the choice of the name Sabellicus and the designation of "in hydra arte secundus" (i.e., the Sabellicus Numa Pomilius) both identify Faustus with the land that was famous for magic from the time of antiquity.

But the names Sabellicus and Faustus were chosen probably not only because they were appropriate for a learned magus and astrologer. Although these were very unusual names, they were not without precedent. Two well-known contemporary Italian humanists, Marcus Antonius Sabellicus (†1506) and Publius Faustus Andrelinus (†1518), had adopted these names. Both had been students of Pomponio Laetus, who had been the foremost propagator of the idea that humanists should adopt Latin names. In taking over names of famous persons, Faustus must have been aware of the association these names conjured up. Sabellicus was famous primarily as a historian and poet. He hailed from Vicovaro, a village north of Rome in the land of the Sabines.³² The association with the Sabines was undoubtedly the primary factor in the choice of this name.

But Faustus could not really overlook the fact of the humanist's fine scholarly reputation in this consideration. The connection between "Faustus iunior" and his predecessor Publius Faustus Andrelinus is a more compelling one. Andrelinus was better-known in Germany than Sabellicus. He had made a name for himself as a professor of rhetoric and poetry at the University of Paris, where he had started teaching in 1489. Numerous German students, including Beatus Rhenanus, had attended his lectures. Among his friends Andrelinus counted such distinguished humanists as Robert Gaguin and Desiderius Erasmus.[33] Significantly, in 1490 a German theologian reported that Andrelinus also gave lectures on astronomy, specifically on the *De sphaera* of Johannes de Sacrobosco.[34] His interest in the stars also extended to astrology; in 1496 he published a lengthy poem entitled *Faustus de influentia siderum et querela Parisiensis pavimenti*.[35] Gustav Schwetschke's thesis that the fame of Andrelinus inspired Faustus to adopt his name is, therefore, very plausible.[36] By associating himself with Andrelinus, Faustus found another way of boasting about the wide scope of his learning. In addition, the choice of three names may also have been calculated to achieve the same end, since, according to Conrad Celtis, philosophers should have three names.[37]

On the basis of the calling card it seemed to Johannes Virdung that the credentials of Faustus were promising. The card provoked in Trithemius quite clearly the opposite reaction. In the letter to Germanus de Ganay, Trithemius had made it very clear that he was opposed to the methods of the alchemists and astrologers. In other works written at approximately the same time one finds similar attacks on necromancers and other practitioners of traditional magic. For example, in his essay for the Emperor Maximilian, written in 1508, Trithemius singled out necromancy as particularly worthy of condemnation.[38] To be a necromancer implied for Trithemius a pact with the devil. Thus, in the letter to Virdung he condemned the foolishness of one who claimed to be the source of all wisdom in necromancy. But Trithemius did not speak of Faustus' connection with the devil. For Trithemius a man who made such claims was not a philosopher but a fool.[39]

This opinion had, however, a wider basis than just the calling card. Trithemius had information about Faustus from at least three other sources. This fact is impressive evidence for the reputation Faustus had acquired by this time. Although Trithemius insisted that his reports were based on extremely reliable sources ("certissimo...testimonio"), what he proceeded to say of Faustus was actually information very difficult to verify. There is no need to question the basic sincerity of Trithemius or of the persons who reported to him. Nevertheless, one must allow for a certain degree of distortion or corruption in the reports as they passed from the original source to Trithemius. The anecdotes about Faustus indicate that people reacted to him strongly, either positively or negatively. Those who wrote about Faustus show a strong tendency to exaggerate. With a possibility of exaggeration in Trithemius' retelling of these reports, it is not entirely safe to formulate definitive conclusions.

Trithemius first reported what certain priests in Gelnhausen had told him. Since the time lag between the event reported and the report itself must have been a matter of a day or so, and since more than one person reported, this particular anecdote has more credibility than the other two. According to the priests, Faustus "in the presence of many people... claimed to have acquired such comprehensive wisdom and memory that if all the works of Plato and Aristotle with the whole body of their philosophical thought completely disappeared from the memory of man, he himself, through his genius, like another Ezra, could restore all things with a greater degree of eloquence." The phrase "like another Ezra" ("velut Ezras alter") probably represents a parenthetical comment by Trithemius on the extravagant claims to wisdom and memory Faustus had made.[40] The reference is to Ezra's amazing restoration of the destroyed Scriptures, based on a report of Ireneus, recorded in *The Ecclesiastical History* of Eusebius. According to the report, Ezra had the aid of divine inspiration: "... for when the Scriptures had been destroyed in the captivity of the people in the days of Nebuchadnezzar, and the Jews had gone back to their country after seventy years... He (God) inspired Ezra, the priest of the tribe Levi, to restore all the sayings of the prophets who had gone before, and to restore to the people the law given by Moses."[41] In 1508, in another context, Trithemius referred to Ezra's restoration of the Scriptures.[42] This feat was for Trithemius a significant event in the context of his mystical chronology of world history. The importance he attached to Ezra is convincing evidence for the fact that it was he, Trithemius, who made the comparison between Faustus and Ezra. Therefore, the text at this particular point does not permit any inferences about Faustus' beliefs. It implies, rather, that Trithemius' statements reflect to a considerable extent his own ideas, even when reporting the claims of Faustus.

There is, however, a certain consistency in this particular anecdote which makes *most* of the information in it appear credible. The claims of Faustus focused on philosophy, the field in which he had presumably obtained a master's degree. It is significant that the interest indicated here is not characteristic of a purely scholastic background. The typical scholastic philosopher would not have placed Plato before Aristotle; in fact, he might have omitted Plato's name entirely. Scholasticism had not really discovered Plato; thus, the question of restoration makes little sense in reference to him. On the other hand, since the founding of the Platonic academy in Florence, the interest in the works of Plato had become intense. In the 1480s, men like Agricola and Dalberg brought this new movement to Germany. As a student in Heidelberg, Faustus might have been under its influence. Moreover, the report reflects humanistic influence in other ways. The desire to recover lost works of antiquity was, of course, characteristic of humanists. Furthermore, the manner in which Faustus intended to restore the lost writings further identifies him with the goals of the *studia humanitatis:* he would be able to restore the works of Plato and Aristotle with a greater degree of elegance ("cum praestantiore...elegantia"). The striving for an elegant Latin style was still another important trait of humanists. It led them to be very critical of texts used by scholastics. The reported statements express, therefore, a very consistent humanistic bias. It is likely that Trithemius reported the statements faithfully; he would have had no apparent reason for attempting to make Faustus appear a humanist. In fact, the humanistic bias expressed here and Faustus' willingness to discuss Plato and Aristotle (at the risk of being challenged about the depth of his knowledge) tend to confirm what the interpretation of the calling card indicated – that Faustus had academic training and that he liked to appear learned by adopting the customs and clichés of the humanists.

Trithemius then reported that Faustus had been at Würzburg, a city to which the latter had close ties also in the 1530s. "Later, while I stayed in Speyer (i.e., after June 2, 1506), he (Faustus) traveled to Würzburg, and, by the same foolishness, he is reported to have said in the presence of many people that the miracles of Christ were not so amazing; he himself could do all the things Christ had done, as often as and whenever one desired." At the time Trithemius wrote this letter he was in Würzburg, where he had the opportunity to learn about Faustus' visit very soon after it had taken place. Most significant about this report is the boldness of Faustus' boasting. Was he not risking persecution by the Church authorities? It is indeed very likely that Faustus tended to make not only exaggerated claims but also statements that bordered on blasphemy. This was certainly the view of Trithemius who wanted Faustus punished "in order to prevent him from heedlessly and continuously asserting in public things that are contrary to the teachings of the Holy Church." As we will see later, Conrad Mutianus Rufus held the view that the theologians should take up arms against Faustus.

Finally, Trithemius reported on Faustus' activities in Kreuznach. At the time of these events Trithemius was already in Würzburg. But Kreuznach lay very close to Sponheim. Trithemius had reliable friends who kept him informed about events relating to the monastery. Therefore, he probably received his information from someone who had personal experience with the Faustus affair in Kreuznach.

There is no reason to doubt that Franz von Sickingen had been a supporter of Faustus. As Trithemius indicated, in Kreuznach Sickingen served as a district administrator *(balivus)* for the Elector of the Palatinate, and in this capacity he was patron of the local school. His residence was on the nearby Ebernburg. His father Schwiekart von Sickingen had practiced astrology.[43] Franz von Sickingen probably did not obtain a high degree of education. Ulrich von Hutten maintained that he was not knowledgeable in Latin. Sickingen himself claimed that Reuchlin had been his tutor, but this relationship did not entail extensive serious studies.[44] According to a report of a historian of the seventeenth century, Sickingen was dedicated to the study of magic from the time of his youth.[45] Sickingen became famous in later years as a militant supporter of unorthodox causes in the persons of Reuchlin, Hutten, and Luther. Like his father, Franz von Sickingen had great faith in astrology. By a significant coincidence, the astrologer he chose to consult consistently was none other than the Heidelberg astrologer Johannes Virdung von Haßfurt, also in the service of the elector. Dr. Adam Wernher in Heidelberg wrote to Georg Spalatin, a well-known figure of the Reformation movement, that a horoscope by Virdung's own hand, prepared for Sickingen and relating to the year 1523 had been found and that he was sending this text to Spalatin. He noted in his letter that Sickingen was not accustomed to undertaking anything important without Virdung's prognostication and advice. Moreover, he generally acted according to Virdung's recommendation.[46]

This coincidence confirms the accuracy of Trithemius' statement regarding Sickingen's occult interests and helps to characterize the kind of person who, in contrast to Trithemius, was interested in Faustus and expected a great deal of him. Both Sickingen and Virdung were strong believers in the possibility of learning the future from the stars. They were important and famous personalities of their time. They were not shocked by the claims Faustus made. Their approach to the occult sciences was less sophisticated and less exclusive than the natural magic of Trithemius.

The close relationship between Sickingen and Virdung has another possible significance for the biography of Faustus. The time between Faustus' appearance in Kreuznach (towards the end of Lent, 1507) and the time Virdung was awaiting a visit from him in Heidelberg (ca. August, 1507) is not great, considering the fact that Faustus probably resided in Kreuznach for a number of weeks before abandoning his post as teacher there. It is, therefore, possible that Faustus made his way to Heidelberg directly from Kreuznach and that his impending visit to Virdung was inspired by the recommendation of Sickingen.

The most serious accusation Trithemius makes against Faustus is that of sexual perversion. Trithemius writes: "With the most criminal kind of design he soon began to seduce the boys (...mox nefandissimo fornicationis genere cum pueris videlicet voluptari cepit...), and when this behavior came to light, he eluded certain punishment by fleeing." It is extremely difficult to judge to what extent this accusation is justified. The records in Nuremberg call Faustus a sodomite some twenty-five years later. The word sodomite could, of course, refer to homosexuality and thus refer to the alleged seduction of boys in Kreuznach. Or was this reputation the result of exaggerated statements made by Faustus' enemies? The emotional factor involved in questions of sexual behavior makes statements about it, without adequate evidence, difficult to evaluate. It is conceivable that the accusation was based only on a suspicion. An accusation of sexual perversion leveled at a man with bold, unorthodox religious opinions is not surprising. Such an accusation was a commonplace from the time of antiquity. The Romans accused the first Christians of participating in sexual orgies. Throughout the Middle Ages very similar charges were consistently made against heretics and witches. The authorities in Nuremberg referred to Faustus as a sodomite. But since they did not give evidence, we cannot simply assume that the later source is a confirmation of the first one. In both instances overzealous opponents of Faustus may have felt justified in accusing him of acts that men like him were generally thought to commit. It is also conceivable that the later source was based on the story circulated by Trithemius. Despite Trithemius' assurance that his information was reliable, a skeptical view towards the image of Faustus as a sexual pervert is justified.

On the whole, Trithemius' letter to Johannes Virdung is rich in content. Of course, it betrays more with absolute certainty about the author, Trithemius, than about the subject, Faustus. But the personality of Faustus is unmistakably recognizable as a historical figure. The main outlines of the information about him conform to his presumed academic training in Heidelberg and to his activities as revealed in other sources. Above all, the contrast between Trithemius and Faustus emerges with clarity. On the one hand, we see Trithemius as an adherent of natural magic, which was for him a legitimate discipline of philosophy, and as an opponent of popular, unphilosophic magic in the person of Faustus. In the context of his other writings, the attack on Faustus appears as an attempt to assert the superiority of his own position, which was also vulnerable. On the other hand, there is no persuasive evidence that Faustus was interested in the practice of natural magic.[47] Nor did he display any of the mystical tendencies characteristic of Trithemius. Like Trithemius, Faustus promised the achievement of miraculous and sensational deeds. For Trithemius their accomplishment was possible only through philosophic insight. For Faustus the significance of academic learning served primarily to make his promises appear more attractive. Through these promises he was able to impress men like Johannes Virdung and Franz von Sickingen. But his behavior also provoked hostility, as his escape from Kreuznach shows.

Like Pico before him, Trithemius felt that magic was not an occupation for the populace but only for philosophers. He was afraid that in the wrong hands, occult knowledge might be misued. He treated the subject of natural magic with religious reverence. He therefore condemned giving away secrets for profit. Faustus, in contrast, appears to have had little regard for religious sensitivities. For him the practice of astrology and magic had become a means of earning a living, and, like the early humanists, he found it most profitable to wander all over Germany. After 1450, humanists were in demand as interest in the *studia humanitatis* at German universities began to surge. The academic interest in Hermetic writings, cabala, and natural magic came on the heels of this first wave of humanistic influence from Italy. Occult studies acquired legitimacy as a new kind of humanistic activity. In the first decades of the sixteenth century, Faustus monopolized on the renaissance of the occult sciences that became evident in many aspects of life in Germany. Faustus' claim to advanced academic training as a philosopher made his audacious assertions appear more credible.

Trithemius was a prolific writer with a solid humanistic background in classical languages. In contrast, Faustus' academic competence probably did not go far beyond Aristotelian logic or its interpretation according to the scholastic method of the *via moderna*. The fact that he did not leave behind teachings, writings, or publications lends support to Trithemius' claim that Faustus had very little to contribute as a genuine philosopher. In an actual face-to-face confrontation, Trithemius would certainly have shown himself superior to Faustus. At Heidelberg, where Faustus had presumably studied, no student could have been unaware of Trithemius' awesome scholarly reputation. Thus, it is not surprising that Faustus was reluctant to confront him in Gelnhausen.

Yet in one sense, Trithemius and Faustus had much in common. Both philosophers were fascinated by the liberating spirit of the humanistic movement and the excitement of the pioneering spirit of the Renaissance. New horizons of knowledge had become visible in all fields. The two man felt called by fate to reveal and propagate bold new possibilities in the sphere of the occult. Their daring often bordered on heresy. The fact that both of them survived many serious attacks on their reputations was due less to the soundness of their beliefs than to the eagerness of many influential contemporaries to believe that the academic approach to the occult might indeed yield new and miraculous insights.

Faustus and Mutianus Rufus

Rudes admirantur.
Mutianus Rufus on seeing Faustus, letter of
October 3, 1513

The next reliable source of information about Faustus comes in 1513 from Conrad Mutianus Rufus, a fellow humanist and friend of Trithemius. As a canon in Gotha near Erfurt, Rufus appears to have lived the solitary life of a monk, even more so than Trithemius did. His ideals were peaceful study and contemplation. In his tranquil surroundings in Gotha, – where he lived for about twenty-four years, until his death in 1526 – he was able to realize his goals. He had studied in Ferrara and Bologna, and he was undoubtedly a fine teacher, who preferred, however, the role of a host in a small circle of humanist friends to the postition of authority in the university classroom. In contrast to Trithemius, he did not publish. His extant literary works amount to only a few poems and numerous letters, and these have survived mainly because they were copied by his friend Heinrich Urban.[1] Although much has not been preserved, the correspondence gives certain hints about what one might expect from a confrontation between Mutianus and Faustus. The exchange of letters with Trithemius and Reuchlin is particularly significant. Mutianus had great respect for the wisdom and learning of both Trithemius, who was six years his senior, and Reuchlin, who was sixteen years older than he.

In 1500 Mutianus visited Trithemius in Sponheim, where he had a chance to use Trithemius' famous library.[2] Trithemius himself visited Mutianus in Gotha twice.[3] In 1503 Mutianus wrote to Reuchlin, expressing enthusiastic interest in Reuchlin's literary works. Professing to be an ardent follower of Reuchlin's philosophy, Mutianus expresses the hope that Reuchlin will accomplish what Pico had promised to do.[4] These remarks and certain passages of a letter to Trithemius, whom Mutianus addresses as *preceptor ter maximus* (i.e., another Hermes), suggest that Mutianus also engaged in the study of natural magic and cabala in the tradition of Pico.[5] But in the context of his correspondence such an interpretation is speculative. It seems likely that Mutianus' generous praise of Reuchlin and Trithemius was an expression of genuine sympathy with their scholarly ambitions. If he himself pursued the study of natural magic seriously, he was very careful to conceal it.

Like the great majority of his contemporaries, Mutianus believed in astrology.[6] He expressed admiration for Pico, more because of Pico's interpretation of the Psalms than because of his writings on magic.[7] Moreover, when Mutianus referred to Pythagoras, he conjured up praiseworthy customs associated with his school, but he did not reveal any interest in numerology.[8] He explained that he intended to take from poets, philosophers, historians, and lawyers only what was compatible with Christianity. Mutianus considered it impious to want to know more than the Church knew. Trithemius, Reuchlin, and Pico were, of course, much bolder.[9]

Further evidence of Mutianus' reluctance to get involved in occult matters comes to light in his correspondence concerning Reuchlin's famous conflict with Johannes Pfefferkorn. It is well known that *The Letters of Obscure Men*, the famous satire of the Renaissance, originated in the circle of humanists close to Mutianus. His own efforts in support of Reuchlin represented a significant catalyst in the publication of this work.

In 1512 Mutianus wrote of his determination to break his previous silence and to speak out in defense of Reuchlin. But he wrote that he intended to do this primarily by praising the humanist. Characteristically, he relied on the authority of others to demonstrate the excellence of Reuchlin's scholarship. It is, for example, Trithemius who revealed to Mutianus "incredible" stories concerning books Reuchlin had written.[10] The books that Trithemius would have considered incredible were undoubtedly those that dealt with cabala.

If Mutianus preferred not to indulge in the occult, he certainly displayed a very tolerant and sympathetic attitude toward such occupation by others. Early in August, 1513, only a few weeks before he encountered Faustus, Mutianus wrote to Trithemius, recommending his friend Peter Eberbach, who was very much interested in Hebrew studies. Mutianus explained that Eberbach was particularly interested in the "more honorable mysteries of the magicians with which Trithemius was very well acquainted."[11] Mutianus was thus prepared to support the activities of others in the area of natural magic.

In this letter to Trithemius, Mutianus characterized Eberbach in a way that made the outcome of the encounter with Faustus very predictable. Eberbach was, he wrote, modest and of a quiet disposition. He did not wander about, like many vagabonds, boasting to the entire populace.[12] It is precisely a loud boastful vagabond, the opposite of Eberbach, Mutianus recognized in Faustus, whom he met a little later (on October 3, 1513) at an Erfurt inn: "Eight days ago there came to Erfurt a certain soothsayer by the name of Georgius Faustus Helmitheus (Helmstetius?) of Heidelberg, a mere braggart and fool. His claims, like those of all diviners, are idle, and this kind of character has not more weight than a water spider. The ignorant marvel at him. Let the theologians rise against him and not try to destroy the philosopher Reuchlin. I heard him babbling at an inn, but I did not reprove his boastfulness. What is the foolishness of other people to me?"[13]

The impression Faustus made on Mutianus was not unlike the impression he had made on Trithemius. This passage tends to confirm the general reliability of the reports Trithemius had received second-hand. The image of a man who promised people great things through his occult wisdom is consistent.

Mutianus' report is more objective than that of Trithemius. Mutianus was not attempting to promote his own image at the expense of Faustus. Though the purely subjective element is absent, Faustus cannot avoid again becoming a scapegoat, this time to serve the cause of Reuchlin against the theologians. The reference to Faustus is for Mutianus a convenient way of showing that Reuchlin was a genuine philosopher who was unjustly attacked (and whom Mutianus had defended with great vigor in the rest of the letter), while Faustus, practicing the fraudulent occupation of palm reading *(chiromanticus,* cf. the calling card in the letter of Trithemius), deserved to be punished.

Like Trithemius, Mutianus saw philosophy as an occupation for a select few. The attempt to appeal to the masses implied for him the abandonment of philosophy. The observation that the "ignorant marvel at him" shows that Faustus did have a talent for attracting attention, but for Mutianus this talent was morally and philosophically suspect. Despite his silence about the study of natural magic and cabala, Mutianus was clearly on the same side as Trithemius in his opposition to the popular traditional occult practices of his time.

Because it reports with a very high degree of reliability about the personality, behavior and appeal of a man who was very much at home in the nonacademic atmosphere, the testimony of Mutianus is extremely valuable. Nevertheless, Mutianus' view was limited. We know from other sources that Faustus was also able to project a more dignified image. Only from this perspective can one understand Faustus' close relationship to the famous knight Franz von Sickingen, the humanist Daniel Stibar, and the bishop of Bamberg.

Faustus and the Bishop of Bamberg

> X guld(en) geben und geschenckt Doctor Faustus ph(ilosoph)o...
>
> The Account Book of the Bishop, 1520

In 1520 Faustus was in Bamberg, where he prepared a horoscope for Bishop Georg Schenk von Limburg, and he was rewarded by a generous payment of ten gold pieces *(Gulden)*. In this particular instance at least, contrary to the hopes of Trithemius and Mutianus, Faustus was not persecuted by Church authorities; his judgment was deemed valuable at the highest level.

Bishop Georg, who expressed his faith in Faustus' competence, certainly did not have the wide academic background of Trithemius or Mutianus. Nevertheless, he was a man of learning. Born to a noble family in 1470, he registered at the University of Ingolstadt when he was sixteen years old. The university record shows that by this time he was destined for a high Church position, for he was canon of the cathedrals at Bamberg, Würzburg, and Strasbourg.[1] In the summer semester of 1490 he registered at the University of Basel.[2] There is no indication that Georg received any degree from either school, but this is not surprising. Noblemen generally did not submit themselves to the unpleasantries of academic requirements and examinations; they pursued their studies through private tutors. The time of Georg's studies corresponds approximately with those of Faustus in Heidelberg, and they took place when the humanistic movement was on the ascendency at all German universities.

Georg Schenk von Limburg became bishop of Bamberg in 1505. At his court he surrounded himself with learned advisors, and he attracted many humanists and artists to his city.[3] The chief administrative official *(Hofmeister)* was Johann von Schwarzenberg, the author of a new legal code for Bamberg. He also published a number of books in German, including translations of Cicero, prepared with the aid of the humanists Lorenz Beheim und Ulrich von Hutten.[4] Influential figures closely associated with the bishop's court were the brothers Andreas and Jacob Fuchs, both pupils of the famous humanist Crotus Rubeanus, who accompanied them to Bologna. Both Andreas and Jacob were high Church officials in Bamberg.[5] Jacob Fuchs was a supporter of Reuchlin's cause and a particularly close friend of Hutten, who had lived with him in Bologna and who visited him in Bamberg between 1517 and 1520 at least twice. Hutten himself had the opportunity of entering the service of the bishop. In 1518 he dedicated the printed volume of his speech about the Turkish danger to Bishop Georg.[6]

The bishop's court chaplain was Magister Ulrich von Burkhard, a graduate of the University of Leipzig and author of the book *Dialogismus de fide christiana* (1523).[7] The bishop was an enthusiastic patron of the arts, employing Hans Wolf as a regular painter at his court and giving assignments to Loy Hering and Albrecht Dürer.[8] As a bookbinder he employed Johannes Schöner, a highly respected geographer and astrologer, subsequently professor of mathematics and astrology in Nuremberg.

Thus Georg also had access to astrologers in Bamberg. Schöner had been a student at the University of Erfurt and studied astronomy and astrology on his own in Nuremberg. In Bamberg he printed his own books, and he prepared globes that showed the discoveries in the New World. Schöner dedicated his first geographical work, printed on his own press in 1515, to Georg.[9] His later publications dealt primarily with astrology. In spite of the difficulties in his private life (having had a daughter by a concubine and being irregular about his Church duties led to the loss of a benefice in Bamberg), Schöner had the continued support of the bishop.[10]

Another astrologer in Bamberg was Lorenz Beheim, lawyer and humanist, whom Willibald Pirckheimer considered the most learned man in his circle of acquaintances. Beheim had resided and studied in Italy, where he met Reuchlin, and became thus initiated into the secrets of cabala.[11] Beheim's lengthy correspondence with his friend Pirckheimer was dominated by the subject of astrological medicine and alchemy.

There is no record that the bishop ever made use of these academic astrologers in his city. The evidence of his consultation with Faustus suggests that in this one instance, at least, he considered the astrological opinion of Faustus as valuable as theirs. It is also possible that he simply preferred the advice of an outsider in the personal matter of a horoscope.

Hans Müller (perhaps identical with Johannes Müller, an official of the Bamberg ecclesiastical court at this time)[12] recorded in his capacity as treasurer *(Kammermeister)* the payment made to Faustus: "Ten *Gulden* given and presented in appreciation to the philosopher Doctor Faustus, who made a horoscope or prognostication for my master. Paid on the Sunday after Saint Scholastica'a Day (February 10) by the order of His Reverence."[13]

The amount Faustus received is surprisingly high. Hans Wolf received about two *Gulden* for helping Dürer prepare a portrait of Georg. About a year earlier Johannes Schöner had received less than four *Gulden* for binding Erasmus' *De regimine principium*.[14]

The content of Faustus' astrological opinion was not indicated. In the years 1518-19 Georg assigned Loy Hering the task of preparing his epitaph and gravestone. In fact, the bishop was to die soon thereafter, on May 31, 1522.[15] The political crisis, brought about by Luther's conflict with the Church of Rome, was also of great concern to Georg at this time. Many of his advisors leaned strongly in favor of Luther. Lazarus Spengler wrote to Pirckheimer that the bishop was on Luther's side. But in another letter, written just a few weeks later, on November 5, 1520, Spengler, who was threatened by a papal bull, expressed his disappointment in Georg's attitude.[16] Certainly the bishop was careful not to undertake actions that were in conflict with the Roman church. Thus, one might speculate that these matters of special concern might have been the subject of Faustus' astrological opinion.

Faustus' success at the bishop's court is reminiscent of his relationship to Franz von Sickingen, who, like Georg, believed in astrology and rewarded Faustus generously. He recommended Faustus for a position as teacher in Kreuznach. Presumably he also recommended Faustus as an astrologer. This pattern is recognizable later in Faustus' relationship to Philipp von Hutten and Daniel Stibar. Moreover, the evidence about Faustus at Bamberg counterbalances and corrects the one-sided view presented by Trithemius and Mutianus, who presented Faustus as a charlatan and an enemy of the Church. But their view was apparently not shared by all. The ambivalence in the attitudes towards Faustus, already suggested by a careful analysis of their remarks, is confirmed by the actions of the bishop of Bamberg.

Faustus and Kilian Leib

> Am Mitwoch nach viti 1528 ist einem der sich genannt Dr. Jörg Faustus von Heidelberg gesagt, daß er seinen Pfennig anderswo verzehre...
>
> Records of the City of Ingolstadt,
> June 15, 1528

Kilian Leib, the prior of the monastery at Rebdorf (near Eichstätt), takes a unique position among those who had dealings with the historical Faustus. Unlike most of his contemporaries, he had little faith in astrologers; nor did he show interest in magic or other occult sciences. Of course men like Trithemius had argued against the validity of traditional astrology. But their opposition was somewhat deceptive, for they held on to the idea that it was possible to predict future events. Kilian Leib's position was much more sophisticated and modern in that Leib actually attempted to test the accuracy of astrological claims by a persistent method of observation and comparison.

Like Trithemius, he was the recipient of an excellent humanistic education by means of private tutors.[1] He belonged to the Augustinian order and held church positions at an early age. As early as 1502 he corresponded with Willibald Pirckheimer. His friendship with the Nuremberg humanist gave Leib access to a rich library.[2] The correspondence with Pirckheimer shows him to have been an eager reader of classical literature and a scholar who was able to cope with Greek, Hebrew, and Aramaic, as well as Latin.[3] His studies of these languages were in support of his interest in biblical research. But Leib also had a genuine interest in history, reflected in his *Annales maiores* and *Annales minores,* in which he recorded the noteworthy events of his time.

Kilian Leib was greatly disturbed by the events of the Reformation. Luther represented for him the unpardonable heretic of the age, and Pirckheimer's early sympathies with Luther led to a break in their friendship. In January 1528, just before Faustus appeared in the vicinity of Rebdorf, Leib wrote a book in which he tried to show the sources of heresy and the causes of the Reformation.[4] In chapter 6 of this work Leib discusses the influence of the stars and the validity of astrology. His treatment of this subject reveals the basic position that also determined his opinion of Faustus.

Leib's point of departure was the famous conjunction of the sun, moon, and the great planets in the sign of Pisces. It was the great astrological event of the century, made particularly famous by the controversies among astrologers about its meaning. Many prominent astrologers, including Johannes Stöffler, whose book Leib quoted,[5] had predicted an unprecedented, disastrous flood. Kilian Leib kept a particularly careful record of the weather in the year of 1524. Although there was a great deal of rain during that year, no great disaster materialized. This situation led Leib to embark on an intensive treatment of the question whether predictions on the basis of astrology were valid. He displayed his extensive research in meteorology, a field in which he was undoubtedly a pioneer.

For fifteen years Leib had scrupulously recorded the daily state of the weather. At the same time, he tested against this record, beliefs of peasants about weather, and he came to the conclusion that it was impossible to predict weather with certainty.[6] Leib argued, furthermore, that it was not God's will that man should know the future just for the sake of his earthly welfare.[7] The excessive concern about the future was the result of laziness. But Leib did not limit himself to the matter of weather predictions. On the basis of copious references to the authority of the Bible, Pico's tract against astrologers, and personal experience, Leib attacked the entire range of astrological assertions. He rejected the validity of the horoscopes. He claimed that the astrologers were unable to determine the position of the stars accurately.[8] In fact, it was not proper for a Christian to ask about his future as foretold by the stars.[9] About one third of his entire book was dedicated to such arguments, designed to show the unreliability of astrology.

The conclusion of chapter 4 however, takes an unexpected turn. Although the prediction on the basis of the conjunction of 1524 obviously did not materialize in respect to the weather, Leib did discover a possible connection to the Reformation. Thus, he retreated somewhat from his firm stand against astrology to allow the influence of the stars to reveal itself in the case of heresy.[10] Leib relied on the authority of Thomas Aquinas, Bonaventura and Richard of Middletown for his argument. He noted then, in his somewhat abrupt conclusion, that the real change brought about by the position of the stars had been the change in Christian morality, the defection from Christian obedience, the disrespect for the holy sacraments and Christian order.[11]

This polemic against the Reformation and heresy was, of course, the primary purpose of Leib's book. But the resulting distortion of his hitherto consistent treatment of astrology does not change the fact that Leib was basically skeptical of the validity of this "science." The basis of this skepticism was the record Leib kept over the years. The original weather notebook in which Leib had kept this record was discovered by Karl Schottenloher about sixty years ago. Under the notations for July, 1528, Leib wrote down what he had heard about Faustus: "Georgius Faustus of Helmstadt said on the fifth of June that when the sun and Jupiter are in the same constellation, prophets are born (presumably such as he). He asserted that he was the commander or preceptor of the Order of the Knights of St. John at a place called Hallestein on the border of Carinthia."[12]

The parenthetical remark that follows Faustus' astrological assertion reflects the spirit of skepticism that underlay most of Leib's meteorological studies; it implies that Leib did not have faith in what Faustus had to say. This position was consistent with the conclusions of his research, and it was it was not distorted by any polemical intent.

The opinion that the conjunction of the great planets, especially of Jupiter, indicated the birth of heroic men and prophets was widespread among the astrologers of the early sixteenth century. This view went back to Hellenistic and Arabic sources and became very popular in the Renaissance through some of the earliest products of the printing press. Philipp Melanchthon, for example, tried to relate its significance to Luther's horoscope. Thus, what Faustus asserted was consistent with a popular astrological opinion of his time.[13]

Leib recorded the information about Faustus' title as "commander or preceptor of the order of the Knights of St. John" without comment. It appears that he was more interested in Faustus' astrological statement than in the accuracy of his title. The office of "commander or preceptor" was a high position of a religious order whose members were of noble blood. How could Faustus obtain such a position? Was Faustus lying? In support of Faustus' claim one may note that Heilenstein, located today in Northwestern Yugoslavia, did indeed belong to the Knights of St. John under the Grand Prior in Prague. But neither the Prague nor Malta archives of the order have any records or entries that might verify Faustus' assertion.[14]

The presence of Faustus in the area of Rebdorf and the general reliability of the information recorded by Leib are confirmed from another source, which shows that about this time Faustus had been also in Ingolstadt, about twenty kilometers from Rebdorf. The records of the city council of Ingolstadt for June 17, 1528, only ten days after Faustus had made his prediction about the coming of new prophets, contain the following two entries: (In the minutes of the city council) "Today, the Wednesday after St. Vitus Day, 1528. The Soothsayer shall be ordered to leave the city and to spend his penny elsewhere." – (In the record of those banished from the City) "On Wednesday after St. Vitus Day, 1528, a certain man who called himself Doctor Jörg Faustus of Heidelberg was told to spend his penny elsewhere, and he promised not to take vengence on the authorities for this order."[15]

Thus two separate sources, from Rebdorf and Ingolstadt, show independently that the same Georgius Faustus still engaged in the business of predicting future events. These two sources complement each other and provide a more accurate and complete form of his name: Doctor Georgius Faustus of Helmstadt near Heidelberg. As in Kreuznach, he demonstrated in Ingolstadt the side of his personality that caused him to have enemies. This banishment from Ingolstadt does not imply, however, such an extreme transgression as the accusation of sodomy in Kreuznach and, later, in Nuremberg. The reference to the "soothsayer" Faustus suggests that Faustus evoked hostility in connection with his divination.

The memory of Faustus in Ingolstadt did not fade away entirely. In a series of anecdotes, written down some fifty years later, Faustus is found again with the first name of Georgius, and he is described as a lecturer at the University of Ingolstadt.[16] But the fantastic anecdotes destroy the credibility of the information. The university records do not show any sign of Faustus. It is noteworthy, however, that in Ingolstadt the actual first name of Faustus survived longer than it did elsewhere.

Faustus and Joachim Camerarius

> ...dass ich bekennen musz, dasz es der Philosophus Faustus schier troffen hat, dann wir ein fast böszes Jahr antroffen haben...
>
> Philipp von Hutten, letter of January 15, 1540

The link between Joachim Camerarius and the historical Faustus was discovered by Georg Ellinger in the correspondence of Camerarius more than eighty years ago. Ellinger published the relevant excerpt from Camerarius' letter without treating its context in detail. Many articles on the historical Faustus have been written since Ellinger's discovery, and they have repeatedly quoted from or commented on the Faustus-Camerarius relationship. But they have been cursory; they have not gone very far beyond the information provided by Ellinger. The significance of this primary source material has not yet been adequately explained.[1]

There are few reliable sources available for research on the historical Faustus. The Camerarius letter could add a new dimension to this fragmentary information. On the other hand, there is certainly no such lack of information about Joachim Camerarius, one of the most prolific writers of his time. It is the voluminous amount of material that has undoubtedly deterred scholars from attempting to write the comprehensive biography that Camerarius clearly deserves. Camerarius' relationship to Faustus reveals a little considered aspect of his life, and indeed of the entire humanistic movement, of which he was a very important representative: and that is the close relationship between occult science and the *studia humanitatis*.

Camerarius and Faustus crossed paths in the decade of the 1530s. From 1526 to 1535 Camerarius resided in Nuremberg. Faustus, in contrast, led a life of constant wandering, and his activities are difficult to document. In 1520 he was in Bamberg. Some time later he claimed to have lived in Heilenstein. Subsequently he passed through the vicinity of Rebdorf and stayed in Ingolstadt in 1528. In 1532 Faustus came to Nuremberg.

The Nuremberg city records indicate that Doctor Faustus had requested a grant of safe conduct and that on May 10, 1532, the request was refused. Presumably, Faustus had intended to come to Nuremberg from Fürth – where he was staying at the time – and had reason to be concerned about the attitude of the authorities towards him. On the basis of the short entry in the records, it seems that his reputation was the source of concern: "Safe conduct to Doctor Faustus, the great sodomite and practitioner of black magic, now at Fürth, refused. (Signed) Deputy Burgomaster."[2] The crime of sodomy was considered so serious at this time that it merited, if witnessed, capital punishment. In instances of suspicion, however, the general custom was exile from the city.[3] It is evident from the refusal to grant Faustus entry to Nuremberg that some accusations against his normal conduct had reached the ears of the city officials. Four years earlier Faustus had been ejected from the nearby city of Ingolstadt. Admittedly, there is no reference in his case to any sexual misconduct; Faustus is referred to simply as a soothsayer *(Wahrsager)*. Much more incriminating is the famous letter of Johannes Trithemius. Trithemius had a very low opinion of Faustus, and he recounted a very specific instance of sexual misconduct: after having been appointed schoolmaster in the city of Kreuznach Faustus "began to indulge in the most dastardly kind of lewdness with the boys, and when this was suddenly discovered, he avoided by flight the punishment that awaited him."[4] Thus, it seems that the degree of Nuremberg against him was based on the sincere belief on the part of the officials that Faustus was a reprehensible individual because of his morals and because he practiced black magic.

In the case of Faustus' illusive personality the most obvious inference may not, in fact, be totally satisfactory. Every piece of evidence about him reveals that he was a controversial man who inspired not only condemnation but admiration and respect as well. It can be shown, for example, that the motives of Trithemius in his attack on Faustus were not entirely pure; he himself was being accused of practicing black magic at the time he wrote the letter, and he might have exaggerated or distorted facts about Faustus in order to make his own activities appear, by contrast, less reprehensible. Evidence that Faustus' services were appreciated by respectable personages is an entry in the Bamberg records, which shows that Faustus was paid ten gold pieces for preparing a horoscope for the bishop of that city. Later we will consider further proof that Faustus was highly respected by numerous people as an astrologer. It is this profession that most reliable sources ascribe to him. The question arises, then, whether it is possible that the accusations contained in the Nuremberg records were exaggerations or even distortions of the facts. Did the Nuremberg officials perhaps have some unstated reason for not wanting Faustus in their city?

At this time there were many men in Nuremberg engaged in astrology (often referred to as mathematics) and other forms of divination. This unique feature of Nuremberg was the subject of a letter written by Philipp Melanchthon at this time. This city, Melanchthon asserted, had been particularly favorable to the study of astrology and had attracted many learned men who excelled in this field. Among the outstanding mathematicians Melanchthon named were Johannes Müller (Regiomontanus), Johannes Werner, Melchior Pfinzing, and Willibald Pirckheimer. The names Melanchthon chose embrace several generations, beginning in the middle of the fifteenth century.[5] Melanchthon saw the present teachers of the newly founded school in Nuremberg as the successors of this illustrious tradition. With apparent pride (Melanchthon had played a central role in the founding of this school) he stressed that no comparable school could claim as great a number of learned men in this field. Though he mentioned no names, he was clearly referrring specifically to his good friends Johannes Schöner, professor of mathematics, and Joachim Camerarius, professor of Greek and history as well as director of the school.⁶ Both Schöner and Camerarius had been employed by the city since 1526. At the time of Faustus' arrival they were both actively engaged in writing tracts on various astrological matters. Schöner earned a place in the history of astronomy by recognizing the importance of Copernicus and overseeing the first publication of his *De revolutionibus* in 1543. But in contrast to Copernicus, his chief loyalty was to astrology, rather than astronomy. In gratitude to the city for the position he held as mathematician, Schöner resolved to draw up an astrological prediction for Nuremberg for the years 1531 and 1532.⁷ Thus Nuremberg, already so well-endowed in astrology, could expect to gain little by the presence of an outsider of questionable reputation. Just three years before Faustus' arrival, a controversial figure, Paracelsus had been in Nuremberg, and unpleasant disputes had arisen between the local doctors and the outsider.⁸ Was it in the interest of the city, and especially of the academic astrologers Schöner and Camerarius, who were in its services, to allow competition? Was there any need for a nonscholarly astrologer in a city with so many illustrious and presumably reliable men of its own?

These are not questions we can answer on the basis of the scanty evidence presently available. The surviving letters of Camerarius from this period make no mention of Faustus. Nevertheless, the questions posed suggest the hypothesis that the animosity against Faustus, as implied in the city records, was not necessarily motivated strictly by moral considerations but also perhaps, at least to a certain extent, by practical ones. In addition, especially since Hieronymus Holzschuher, the Deputy Burgomaster who issued the reply and refusal to Faustus, is known to have been an acquaintance of Camerarius, there exists the possibility that Camerarius was aware of Faustus' petition.⁹ In light of the subsequent astrological competition between Camerarius and Faustus, this line of speculation can be justified because it is possible that the initial encounter took place in some form at this time in Nuremberg.¹⁰

The nature of the astrological competition that took place later between Camerarius and Faustus comes to light primarily in the writings of Camerarius. There is an unusual wealth of material relating to astrology and other forms of divination, and for no other period of the life of Camerarius are such materials so extensive as they are for the decade between 1530 and 1540.

One significant source of Camerarius' interest in astrology was Johannes Schöner, to whom he referred as a friend.¹¹ But his intimate friend Melanchthon undoubtedly exerted an even greater influence in this connection. Melanchthon had studied astrology and astronomy at the University of Tübingen under Johannes Stöffler, one of the most respected astrologers of the time.[12] At the University of Wittenberg he told his own students repeatedly that astrology was not only a legitimate academic subject but also a significant tool in the administration of the affairs of state.[13] Camerarius came under the influence of the older Melanchthon as early as September, 1521, when he himself started teaching at the University of Wittenberg.[14] A close friendship developed between the two scholars. To the generally acknowledged list of common interests, which included classical languages and literatures, religion and politics, one must add astrology. The characterization of the Camerarius correspondence for the decade of the 1530s is applicable to the Melanchthon correspondence: Melanchthon's letters also display a very intense interest in astrological information relating to the possible outcome of the great religious and political conflicts of their time; most letters he addressed to Camerarius treated such astrological problems.

Melanchthon rationalized his firm faith in the value of astrology by referring to the high esteem it enjoyed among the great men of antiquity. He deplored the neglect that this field suffered in later ages, and he credited two Germans, Georg Peuerbach and Johannes Müller, with having brought about its renaissance.[15] If Melanchthon recognized astrology as a part of the ancient wisdom that was very much worth rediscovery and renewal, such a humanistic attitude or approach was even more characteristic of Camerarius. Having gained recognition as one of the outstanding scholars of Greek studies, Camerarius began to apply his scholarly abilities to the service of astrology and other occult sciences. In 1532 he edited and translated Greek works by Hephaestion of Thebes, Hermes Trismegistus, and Vettius Valens, under the title of *Astrologia*. These works contained practical information about stars and planets relevant to making predictions. In the introductory letter of Andreas Perlach, professor of mathematics in Vienna, Camerarius explained that he had based his editions on materials in a manuscript volume that had been written almost entirely by Regiomontanus' own hand. The valuable books of Regiomontanus were in the possession of Johannes Schöner.[16] From this library, Camerarius was also to publish the commentary of Theon of Alexanderia on the astronomical writings of Ptolemy. A very significant product of his astrological studies was the edition of the Greek text of the *Tetrabiblos* of Ptolemy with notes and a translation for Books I and II and a partial translation of Books III and IV. The Nuremberg edition of 1535 was the very first printing of the Greek *Tetrabiblos*.[17] This scholarly work on astrology ran parallel to Camerarius' other humanistic activities in editing (and in some cases also translating) works of Homer, Aesop, Sophocles, Theocritus, Galen, Cicero, Quintilian and Macrobius, all in the 1530s.

A phenomenon that aroused great excitement among astrologers of this time was the appearance of a comet, known today as the famous Halley's comet, in August and September of 1531. Even Luther, who was generally very critical of astrology, felt that the comet indicated the advent of significant events. Both Johannes Schöner and Joachim Camerarius wrote extensively on its significance.[18] The letters of Melanchthon in Wittenberg at this time reveal the keen interest the comet evoked. He reported to Camerarius on seeing the comet for the first time on August 18. His subsequent letters consistently referred to it. In one letter Melanchthon deplored the lack of news about the comet; in other letters he requested that friends send him the opinion of other astrologers (especially that of Schöner); then he complained that the comet was not visible, and to Camerarius he sent the opinion of a Polish astrologer concerning the same celestial phenomenon.[19] The immediate reaction of Camerarius himself is revealed in a letter to his close friend in Würzburg, Daniel Stibar: on October 8, 1531, Camerarius reported that the comet had been observed for more than fourteen days. After describing its path, he ventured the interpretation that it would undoubtedly bring pestilence.[20] What such celestial phenomena might signify was the central theme of a book Camerarius wrote during the subsequent months. In this work Camerarius assembled the opinions of ancient writers on comets, demonstrating that these phenomena were always thought to have unfortunate implications. Moreover, Camerarius showed that the views of antiquity were supported by the evidence of history. Providing an amazing wealth of information Camerarius again displayed the wide scope of his acquaintance with classical literature. Melanchthon received the manuscript of *Norica sive de ostentis,* as Camerarius called his work, in late December, 1531, and promised to see to its publication, which then actually took place in Wittenberg during the fall of the following year.[21]

Camerarius also engaged in a much more practical kind of astrology. The correspondence of Johannes Apel, friend of Camerarius in Nuremberg and former chancellor to the duke of Prussia, reveals something about his involvement in prognostication and his particular approach to it. After Camerarius had prepared a horoscope for Albrecht, duke of Prussia, he asked Apel to send it to the duke, together with predictions for the coming three years, from 1535 to

1537. Apel praised Camerarius as a great mathematician who had prepared horoscopes for many princes. Apparently he feared, however, that the astrological work of his friend might be subjected to criticism at the Prussian court, for he warned the duke not to show the horoscope to Poliander, Albrecht's court chaplain. Camerarius, he wrote, employed a different method, based on the works of Ptolemy, Carion and others. If help were needed to interpret the predictions, Apel suggested that one should consult the old canon in Frauenburg, who was none other that the famous Copernicus.[22] Apel did not indicate why Albrecht should mistrust Poliander, who is known to have had an active interest in astrology.[23] Poliander was a Lutheran theologian and trusted advisor of Albrecht, and Apel, recently chancellor to the duke, was certainly well acquainted with him. Perhaps Apel felt that Poliander lacked the necessary background and experience in academic astrology based on Ptolemy rather than on medieval authorities. These were qualifications, after all, that he recognized and praised in Camerarius. On the other hand, Carion was a widely recognized astrologer, who served Albrecht not only in this capacity but also as an advisor and a diplomat. Like Melanchthon and Schöner, Carion had learned his astrology from Johannes Stöffler in Tübingen. Melanchthon had great respect for Carion's astrological views, and he relayed them to Camerarius.[24] Copernicus was, of course, primarily an astronomer. But he dabbled in astrology, as various notes in his manuscripts prove. He made excerpts from Ptolemy's *Tetrabiblos* and he collected other astrological data. The fact that the astrological views of Camerarius were thought to be safe in the hands of scholarly "astrologers" like Carion and Copernicus, who were well acquainted with the authorities of classical antiquity, and not safe in those of a man whose academic training was primarily in theology, is not surprising. There were other instances, notably the case of the astrological competition with Faustus, when Camerarius felt the need to stress the superiority of his scholarly kind of divination.

The first of the known "confrontations" between Camerarius and Faustus concerned an expedition that Philipp von Hutten, the cousin of the humanist Ulrich von Hutten, undertook to the New World. Both astrologers made predictions on the future of this expedition. Both men became interested in the fate of the Hutten expedition, and at least from the perspective of Camerarius, there is ample evidence to show how this interest originated and developed.

The friendship of two Catholics, Daniel Stibar and Moritz von Hutten, was instrumental in bringing the Lutheran Camerarius into the orbit of Faustus. Camerarius and Stibar became close friends when they were both young students at the University of Erfurt. Here they came under the influence of humanists like Eobanus Hesse, Crotus Rubeanus, and Mutianus Rufus.[25] It was at Erfurt that Stibar became proficient in the Greek language, and his keen interest in classical studies strengthened his bond of friendship with Camerarius. Later, Stibar followed Camerarius to Wittenberg, where he also became a friend of Melanchthon. Despite his closeness to Lutheran scholars, Stibar remained faithful to the Catholic Church. In 1526 he was in Italy, and in the following year he registered at the University of Basel. Here he was joined by Moritz von Hutten, who, like Stibar, had close ties to Würzburg.[26] At Basel Stibar and Hutten studied law and both soon found access to the much coveted company and circle of Erasmus of Rotterdam and Boniface Amerbach. Stibar became an especially faithful pupil and good friend of Erasmus; he lived for a time in the famous humanist's household. When Erasmus moved to Freiburg in 1529, Stibar and Hutten followed him there. In April of 1530 Stibar was made canon in Würzburg and returned there to become councillor to Bishop Conrad von Thüngen.[26] In the following years Stibar and Erasmus kept in touch through correspondence. Hutten went to Eichstätt, where he was to become bishop of the Catholic Church in 1539.[27] During the 1530s Camerarius, Stibar, and Hutten remained close through a very diligent correspondence and numerous reunions. The divergent religious views of the Lutheran Camerarius appeared to be no hindrance; they had no difficulty in overlooking them because of their hope of a religious reconciliation. They shared this hope for the sake of humanistic studies in Germany, and they believed that the realization of their common hopes depended on the political successes of the Emperor. There was a genuine interest in exchanges of views on scholarly questions. Camerarius had encouraged Moritz von Hutten, for example, to take an interest in the literary remains of his famous cousin, Ulrich von Hutten. Ulrich's dialogue *Arminius* was in fact published by Moritz in Nuremberg in 1529.[28] Camerarius frequently consulted with Stibar on his publications, asking him to examine the accuracy of his texts or interpretations.[29] The three men also shared an interest in astrology and this interest was closely tied to their common scholarly and political interests.[30] When Moritz's brother set off for the New World, a question of personal pride and concern intensified their contacts with each other, and they turned to astrology as a matter of natural course. After Hutten's departure the correspondence and meetings of the friends reflects their concern about the fate of the venture.[31]

Camerarius had been acquainted with Philipp von Hutten as early as 1529. In the fall of that year Hutten had passed through Nuremberg and stopped at Camerarius' house to report on the health of his brother Moritz.[32] Philipp himself had no university education. He had been brought up close to the imperial court under the tutelage of the Duke Heinrich von Nassau, one of the advisors of Charles V. Consequently, Philipp lived and traveled a great deal abroad, especially in Spain; letters of November 1531 indicate that he also traveled in Germany on missions for the duke. When he resolved in 1534 to take part in the expedition of the Welser family to the New World he was still in the service of the duke.[33] Hutten's description of the expedition begins with his departure from Spain; in this context he did not refer to either Camerarius or Faustus.

In a book entitled *Erratum*, published in 1535, Camerarius expressed his special interest in the fate of Hutten's expedition. This strange work was the product of a quarrel with Erasmus.[34] Having been accused by Erasmus of committing errors, Camerarius defended himself by showing that others, including Erasmus, were guilty of similar failings. Thus, the main prose section presents a panorama of mistakes made by great authors of all time, from Homer to Erasmus. To this main prose text Camerarius appended three lengthy poems relating to the conceptions of classical antiquity about winds, stars, and various forms of prognostication. The dedications are noteworthy: the first poem was dedicated to Moritz von Hutten, and the other two were written for Daniel Stibar. The introductory section of the first poem treats the future of the Hutten expedition.

Unfortunately, the information provided is not very specific and does not shed much light on the nature or circumstances of the original prediction. Lines 5 and 6 appear to indicate that Camerarius had examined the question whether the time was propitious for the undertakings of Hutten.[35] This distich suggests that he had made the prediction before Hutten set off for America on October 19, 1534. The poem dwells at length on the glory that Philipp will bring to his nation and his family. Camerarius alludes to his audience with Charles V, which is known to have taken place before his departure on August 22, 1534.[36] Finally, the poet stresses his ardent desire for a good outcome of the expedition.[37] Camerarius made a more significant reference to the Hutten expedition in a letter dated May 18, 1536, addressed to Daniel Stibar. He published this letter as a preface in a book containing the following three items: 1) *Commentarius captae Urbis ductore Carolo Borbonio*, 2) *Carolus sive Vienna Austriaca*, 3) *Carolus sive Tunete*. The first item is an anonymous historical account of the sack of

Rome by imperial forces in 1527. The text is followed by two poems of Camerarius: one praising the emperor for his role as savior of Vienna against the attacks of the Turks and the other for his role in the successful expedition against Tunis.[38] All these works were sympathetic to the cause of the Emperor, the poems of Camerarius with much greater emotion than the anonymous prose text. This enthusiastic dedication to the cause of Charles V comes to light in many writings of Camerarius during this decade, and his letter to Stibar treats this theme at length. The devotion to the Emperor went hand in hand with a great interest in interpreting the astrological signs that had bearing on his future. At least as early as 1532 Camerarius consulted Melanchthon on the horoscope of Charles V.[39] A prediction about the success of the Hutten expedition, which was to add to the glory of the Emperor, follows directly upon the discussion of prophecies concerning Charles V. In Camerarius' eyes the stars and fortunes of Hutten and Charles V were closely linked.

Camerarius prefaced his generous and confident forecasting with remarks that betray some insecurity. He was not entirely sure whether his friend Stibar had sufficient trust in Camerarius' predictions. He wrote "Don't think that one should accept any divinations of astrologers or soothsayers with greater faith than those of men who discovered the essence of prophecy, not steeped in some kind of superstition, but endowed with a certain instinct and divine power."[40] These words are clearly calculated to anticipate and counteract the possibility that Stibar might consult an astrologer or soothsayer who lacked the ancient secret of prophecy. In a letter that he wrote only three months later Camerarius warned Stibar about the wrong kind of divination. He did so by criticizing the superstitious practices of one particular astrologer: Stibar's trusted friend Faustus.[41] Camerarius knew that Stibar consulted Faustus in astrological matters. This fact makes it quite likely that Camerarius' earlier general warning about unreliable astrologers or soothsayers was really directed primarily against Faustus. Thus, in a manner similar to the instructions relayed to Duke Albrecht, Camerarius distinguished his approach to divination from other approaches. Again the emphasis was on learning. In both instances his approach is revealed to have been basically humanistic: the solution to problems of discovering the future lay in a return to the sources of wisdom in antiquity.

In the letter to Stibar, Camerarius gave a demonstration of a unique aspect of his approach to divination. His admitted purpose was to strengthen Stibar's faith in the Emperor.[42] In this he resorted not to astrology, but to the ancient *sortes Homericae* and *sortes Virgilianae*. With *sortes* Camerarius understood a method of divination commonly used in antiquity, which entailed the opening of a Homeric or Virgilian text at random and interpreting the passage thus encountered. Camerarius reported to Stibar that the Homeric *sortes* (by the implication of the context, drawn by Camerarius himself) were extremely favorable to Charles V and that Stibar need not have any doubts about the outcome of the Emperor's struggles: "His honour is from Zeus, and Zeus Allwise cares for him." (*Iliad*, II, 197).[43]

Camerarius reported, furthermore, on the Virgilian *sortes* which were drawn when Charles had been just a boy. The result was equally favorable: "Because of his arrival even now the Caspian kingdoms and the Scythian land dread the divine oracles, and the mouths of the sevenfold Nile are alarmed." (*Aeneid*, VI, 788-800).[44]

In reporting these favorable omens Camerarius took pains to stress his disapproval of "vulgar" prophecies, whereas he referred, in contrast, to the learning of the men who had been responsible for the Virgilian *sortes*. Learning, however, was not all that was required in divination; there also had to be, according to Camerarius, the gift of instinct and divine power. Camerarius apparently believed that he himself possessed this enviable gift.

Many prophecies about Charles V were in circulation at this time, the most famous of which was a prophecy by Joachim de Fiore († ca. 1202), the prophecy previously applied to the Hohenstaufen and earlier Habsburg emperors, and now to Charles V.[45] Quite possibly Camerarius was referring to this tradition when he expressed to Stibar his reluctance to explicate "vulgar" and older prophecies. These, according to Camerarius, were very well known to Stibar.

The belief in prophecy was one of the remaining close links between medieval and Renaissance thought.[46] Camerarius' thinking was not unique in this area, but he deviated from his contemporaries by basing his visions on Greek divination. He obviously felt that his wide classical learning endowed his predictions with a validity lacking in the pronouncements of "vulgar" astrologers or soothsayers such as Faustus.

After presenting his favorable view of the Emperor's future Camerarius turned to the expedition of Philipp von Hutten: "These things, my Daniel, you will hopefully share with our (Moritz von) Hutten, whose brother Philipp, a youth destined for fame, having returned from the Indian expedition, we perceive to be leading a number of troops to the Emperor. For his most praiseworthy undertakings we prayed to insure a favorable turn of fortune. This he had indeed achieved with such brave and great spirit beyond his age that in this matter the very inconstant goddess appears to be steadfast. For whatever happens, I desire and prophesy an entirely propitious outcome."[47]

Camerarius perceived or foresaw the triumphant return of Philipp von Hutten to the Court of Charles V. The eagerness with which Camerarius looked forward to Hutten's success is not unlike his great desire for the political success of the Emperor. His optimistic evaluation of the future appears in retrospect to have been influenced, at least in these two instances, by political as well as personal interests. This appearance does not exclude the possibility that Camerarius made a sincere attempt, by astrological or other means to ascertain whether the conditions for the Hutten expedition were favorable.

Faustus saw the future of the expedition in a much different way. The evidence that he was also consulted is found in the letters Hutten wrote from the New World. On January 16, 1540, Philipp von Hutten wrote a lengthy report about his experiences to his brother, and at this time he referred also to Faustus: "Here you have a little about all the provinces so that you may see that we are not the only ones who have been unfortunate in Venezuela up to this time; that all the aforementioned expeditions which left Sevilla before and after us perished within three months. Therefore I must confess that the philosopher Faustus hit the nail on the head, for we struck a bad year."[48] Thus, Faustus may be identified as the author of a prognostication for the year of Hutten's departure from Spain in 1534. Faustus had judged this year to be unfavorable for the expedition, undoubtedly on the basis of the constellation of the stars at that time. Hutten's words imply respect for the accurate prediction Faustus had made. The fact that Faustus was the superior astrologer in this particular instance was confirmed, furthermore, by the succeeding events. Philipp von Hutten remained in Venezuela for six more years of frustrating and unsuccessful explorations, and finally he fell victim to the fighting among competing explorers. In 1546 he was killed by a Spaniard. Camerarius wrote the epitaph for Philipp. It was incribed on the latter's gravestone in the chapel Mariasondheim near Würzburg, and here an elaborate relief shows the kneeling figures of Moritz and Philipp before a crucifix in the foreground with the story of the tragic death of Philipp in the background.[49]

There are strong indications that Würzburg was the place where Faustus had been consulted. The same letter from Hutten that confirms the accuracy of the prognostication by Faustus refers to this city a number of times. Hutten asked his brother to give special greetings to Daniel Stibar and, similarly, to all his good comrades at the Würzburg Court.[50] In 1536 Camerarius wrote Stibar that he had received a package of letters from Philipp and that these were to be taken care of by Stibar.[51] Philipp von Hutten himself had been born in Arnstein, about twenty kilometers north of Würzburg. Würzburg was, consequently, a place that Hutten had visited on numerous occasions, and Daniel Stibar was a mediator to his acquaintances there. Since it is known from a letter of Camerarius that Faustus was a good friend of Stibar's, it is reasonable to conclude that the latter was responsible for soliciting the help of Faustus in this matter.[52]

In 1536 Camerarius was prepared to match another prediction with that of Faustus. The fate of the Hutten expedition was still unknown, but Camerarius had the fate of that expedition very much in mind when he wrote to Stibar on August 13. Here Camerarius revealed that his new book *Commentarius*, with its reference to the success of the Hutten expedition, was being dedicated to Stibar.[53] At the same time he wrote of Faustus: "When the moon stood in Pisces in opposition to Mars, on August 4, I endured a very difficult night. Your Faustus is responsible for the fact that I discuss these matters with you. I wish he had taught you something more about this art, rather than inflating you with the wind of most fruitless superstition or holding you in suspense with I don't know what kind of tricks. But pray, what does he tell us at last? And what new things? I know that you have diligently inquired about everything. Is the Emperor not going to be victorious? That is, in fact, what will have to happen."[54]

This important passage reveals, first of all, that Faustus was a close friend of Stibar's. This fact is clearly implied by the phrase "your Faustus," but it is strongly reinforced by the contention that Faustus was a mentor whom Stibar trusted and consulted often. Camerarius did not consider the learning imparted by Faustus to Stibar worthwhile, and he proceeded to illustrate what was, in his opinion, a legitimate area of study. Camerarius related an astronomical oberservation (moon in Pisces in opposition to Mars) he had made a few days before. Astrological texts such as the *Tetrabiblos* indicate that Mars is a maleficent planet, and if it enters into a crucial relationship (e.g., opposition) with the moon (which has particular significance in matters of health) the result is adverse.[55]

Camerarius felt that he could demonstrate very simply what a true application of astrology involved. Like Melanchthon, he assumed that stars, because of their position, influenced events on earth and that the principles of astrology were based on their "physical" effects. In this case, Camerarius tested and proved to his own satisfaction the reliability of one such astrological principle. He compared the view of authoritative astrologers that "Mars in opposition to the moon" produced negative results with his own personal experience of great physical pain one night under precisely those astrological conditions. This correspondence confirmed to Camerarius the correctness of the astrological principle. In his work on comets (1532) Camerarius used a similar kind of logic in showing that certain celestial events always had unfortunate effects. When Johannes Schöner predicted the future of Nuremberg for the years 1531 and 1532 he also employed the same "scientific" approach; he used his knowledge about the position of the stars during 1348, 1449, and 1502 (times when Nuremberg experienced great difficulties) in order to analyze the prospects for the immediate future.[56]

On the other hand, according to Camerarius, Faustus employed deceptive tricks. This judgment about Faustus may not have been without some justification; at least two other scholarly men, Johannes Trithemius and Mutianus Rufus, believed that Faustus was a theatrical and boasting deceiver. Trithemius reported that Faustus had claimed to be able to restore the works of Plato and Aristotle, if they were lost to the memory of man, and that he could perform miracles like the ones Christ had performed. Mutianus Rufus observed Faustus in an inn as people were marvelling at his words, though he himself considered the man a braggart and a fool. We may assume that the considerably older Faustus was able to create a more dignified impression on a man like Daniel Stibar. But this would have been consistent with the histrionic talents that Faustus undoubtedly possessed. What tricks he used to impress Stibar are not known. That he had considerable experience as an astrologer is established from other sources. Whatever his approach to divination, from the point of view of Camerarius it appeared insincere, unorthodox and unscientific. Camerarius was confident that in a competition against his scholarly approach to divination such an approach would fail.

Camerarius was willing to put his belief to a test on the question of the Emperor's war with France. The study of the Emperor's political future was for him by far the most time-consuming astrological concern in the 1530s and 1540s. He was examining this matter at least as early as 1532, when he obtained a horoscope of Charles V from Melanchthon.[57] His involvement became particularly intense in 1536 when another great confrontation between Charles V and Francis I appeared imminent. It is at this time that Camerarius was willing to test his prediction of success for Charles V against what he suspected was a contradictory assessment on the part of Faustus.

On the day that Camerarius wrote to Stibar about Faustus, August 13, 1536, he also wrote to his friend Eoban Hesse: "The news about the French war holds everyone in suspense. It will undoubtedly cause a great and unforeseen revolutionary change. But this 'I do not say in prophecy, but judging from the state of things,' as the Tiresias of Euripides says, so that you won't ridicule me as an astrologer, as you are accustomed to doing."[58] Although Camerarius did not disclose to Hesse the most significant feature of his astrological prediction, the impending victory of Charles V, he hinted at this clearly by speaking of a momentous event in the future. His words here reflect the excitement with which he anticipated the coming political events. But in this instance he implied that his expectations were based on a common-sense evaluation of the state of affairs. That such an evaluation would correspond with the result of his astrological analysis is another illustration of a trait characteristic of Camerarius: That his prediction of future events tended to confirm his previous beliefs or desires.

As Camerarius perceived these developments with apparent confidence he was also plagued by anxieties and fears. He confided to Stibar that there was nothing he feared more than the possibility of an upheaval in Germany. A few days later he observed that the present war might be the signal of very great upheavals.[59] Such concern and inconsistency were characteristic of Camerarius, who had been forced to endure many political changes and disappointments during his lifetime. His prayers, predictions, and fears about the future triumphs of Charles V reflected his desperate and somewhat uncertain faith in the emperor as agent of peace and reconciliation in Germany.

It is not known what Daniel Stibar replied to the question put to him about Faustus. Almost all of his letters to Camerarius have been lost.[60] That he did write to Camerarius very soon is evident. Melanchthon was visiting Camerarius in Tübingen towards the end of September. From there he wrote to Stibar, thanking him for the kind words and greetings. Melanchthon wrote to Stibar about his hope of reconciliation in Germany and the important role of moderation Stibar might play in this cause. He asked Stibar to forward best wishes to Moritz von Hutten. This letter, dated September 29, 1536, did not contain any mention of Faustus.[61] But since the matter relating to Faustus was a problem of personal concern primarily to Camerarius, this omission is not surprising.

The fact that Stibar was concerned about the French war at this time is indicated in a letter he wrote to Erasmus. He mentioned the Emperor's attack upon France and supposed, with some exaggeration, that the thunder of guns was undoubtedly audible in Basel. In fact, this letter never reached Erasmus; before it could have been sent off, the news of Erasmus' death must have reached

Stibar. The letter was copied by Camerarius, and it survives in his manuscript collection as the only existing copy.[62] Given the evidence of Stibar's concern about the war, it is quite conceivable that he consulted Faustus on this matter and then relayed the requested information to Camerarius.

Melanchthon probably discussed with Camerarius the latter's astrological competition with Faustus. His correspondence with Camerarius before and after this visit was very much dominated by astrological concerns and anxieties about the French war. The letter that Melanchthon wrote in July, just before his visit, was devoted entirely to astrology. It was very defensive in tone, for some unnamed people had been attacking and mocking him for his excessive devotion to this field. It is known that Luther was his most prominent critic in this regard.[63] In 1537 he and Camerarius edited a book entitled *Mathematicarum disciplinarum tum etiam astrologiae encomia*. The work included three lengthy letters by Melanchthon on the justification of astrology as a praiseworthy academic subject.[64] The final item was the astrological poem *Phaenomena* by Camerarius, published once before in 1535 and dedicated to Stibar.[65] This book was published in Strasbourg, and it was perhaps the fruit of Melanchthon's meeting with Camerarius in Tübingen. The French war was of no less interest to Melanchthon than to Camerarius. While he was still visiting Camerarius he wrote to a friend about the current discussion of the French affairs in Tübingen.[66] In subsequent letters to Camerarius, Melanchthon repeatedly referred to this topic. On October 11, 1537, Melanchthon asked Camerarius to examine his French horoscope and to inform him of his opinion about the coming year.[67] Under these circumstances the astrology of Faustus, which was very much on the mind of Camerarius, undoubtedly came up in the conversations of the two close friends.

It is ironic that Melanchthon, who had an excellent opportunity to obtain first-hand information about Faustus, left behind totally unreliable reports. In the lecture notes recorded by his students there are two references to Faustus: one that refers to an unsuccessful attempt in Venice by Faustus to fly and the other that claims that Faustus had devoured another magician in Vienna.[68] Numerous historians have attached great value to the Faustus anecdotes of Melanchthon as recorded by Johannes Manlius, in spite of the fact that they were published in 1562, many years after the death of Faustus, at a time when the legends about him were already widespread. The fantastic stories related here are just as unreliable as the statements previously mentioned. In this collection of anecdotes some information survives concerning the views of Faustus on the

French war: "... The same magus Faustus, a most shameful beast and sewer of many devils, vainly boasted that all the victories that the imperial armies won in Italy were achieved through his magic. This was a malicious lie. I say this for the sake of young people, so that they do not instantly assent to such idle men."[69] Whatever truth might at one time have been at the source of these remarks, it did not fare well in the superstitious hands of Melanchthon and Manlius, whose exaggerations and polemics distorted it beyond recognition.

It is unknown whether Faustus was correct in his assessment of the French war, but it is clear that Camerarius was wrong, just as he had been wrong in the case of Philipp von Hutten. The great war he had expected did not develop. In July of 1536 Charles V invaded the Provence and reached the gates of Marseilles, but after an unsuccessful siege he retreated and finally gave up the entire venture. Camerarius was reluctant to admit defeat. His belief in astrology remained unshaken, and he continued to make predictions on the French war in the following years. In 1538 he was again, mistakenly, expecting a big war in France during the coming year; once more he invoked the words of Tiresias in claiming that he was not really making a prophecy, which he was leaving to others, but simply judging "from the state of things."[70] His expectation did not materialize. In 1542 there were rumors of a war between Charles V and Francis I, and it appears that by this time Camerarius had become considerably more hesitant about making predictions, for he did not offer any opinion at all. This did not mean that he had given up.[71] Once when asked for information about his prognostications of the French war, Camerarius admitted in his reply (undated, probably after 1552) that conjectures about individual events were uncertain.[72] During the 1540s his comments on the political situation began to appear more and more pessimistic and fatalistic. His admiration for the Emperor tended to fade; the Schmalkaldic War, in which Charles fought against Lutheran princes, dealt his former devotion a very painful blow.[73]

To the end of his life Camerarius remained faithful to his keen interest in the occult sciences: in 1559 he published a work on comets *(De eorum quae cometae appelantur)*, and before he died he had completed a work on the various forms of divination in antiquity *(Commentarius de generibus divinationum)*, published posthumously in 1576 by his son Ludwig Camerarius.

This aspect of Camerarius' work and, in particular, his competition with Faustus are reflections of a significant phenomenon: the great flourishing of the occult sciences. About his confrontation with Camerarius Faustus left behind only a few traces. Reliable documents about his earlier life, however, make it possible to reconstruct his approach to divination and thus show how it contrasted to that of Camerarius. The calling card Faustus sent to two different persons in 1507 lists the occult sciences he was proud to practice. Faustus did not hesitate to approve a considerable number of occult practices, most of which required no academic training at all. Furthermore, the calling card and the testimony of Johannes Trithemius indicate that Faustus was interested not just in predicting future events but also in performing magic. By embracing such a wide scope of occult practices Faustus was different from Camerarius, who, scorning magic, placed his faith primarily in astrology. He focused his efforts on mastering this field by studying the Greek sources. On the authority of classical sources he was inclined to accept the validity of such divinatory practices as drawing lots *(sortes)*.

The primary motivation of Camerarius in resorting to divination appears to have been political. Like Melanchthon and other contemporaries, Camerarius hoped to become a wiser and more influential participant in political affairs by being able to forecast events. Through publication he made sure that his pronouncements received wide circulation. In fact, it appears that men like Camerarius evaluated contemporary occurrences more on the basis of a hypothetical future than on the basis of past experience. Camerarius' view of Charles V as a heroic savior of Germany was certainly based more on the hopes that the *sortes* and the stars raised than what the stern facts of the emperor's policy towards the Protestants warranted. Ultimately, the astrological politics of Camerarius reveal a desperate hope for religious peace under the leadership of the emperor. In this he was not unlike Melanchthon, who sided with the Italian Roman Catholic bishop, Luca Gaurico, in resolving the problem of Luther's horoscope, in spite of the fact that the results were not friendly to the cause of Reformation and necessitated a revision of the information provided by Luther's mother about the time of the reformer's birth. Astrology, like the classics, thus offered a neutral territory and afforded a common meeting ground where religious and political differences could be ignored and temporarily forgotten.[74] Seen in a wider context, the astrological politics of Camerarius represent a phenomenon also characteristic of the many prophecies made towards the end of the fifteenth century: the channeling of deep-seated political frustrations into visions of the future because at this time social and political institutions afforded no other apparent way of expressing them. In this way the confrontation of Camerarius and Faustus testifies to a significant historical phenomenon. In the records of his activities there is no indication that Faustus was motivated by humanistic or political ideals. He prepared his horoscopes for monetary reward, as the Bamberg records show. In the area of astrology Faustus was not as knowledgeable about the original Greek sources as was Camerarius. But Faustus did know how to cast a horoscope, and to what extent classical sources actually aided Camerarius in arriving at accurate results is a debatable question. In one case, at least, the academic astrology of Camerarius failed. Perhaps one should not attach much significance to the question of superiority in the competition between these two men. Both men had in common the historically important distinction of having contributed greatly to the revival and prospering of the occult sciences in the sixteenth century.

IV

THE DEATH OF FAUSTUS

> *(Faustus) ist ein alter Mann worden...*
> Zimmerische Chronik

The *Zimmerische Chronik*, written by Froben Christoph von Zimmern and his secretary Johannes Müller, is the earliest report of Faustus' death, and it presents a very lively and dramatic account:

> That the practice of such art (soothsaying) is not only godless but in the highest degree dangerous is undeniable, for experience proves it, and we know what happened to the notorious Faustus. After he had practiced during his lifetime many marvels about which a special treatise could be written, he was finally killed at a ripe old age by the evil spirit in the seigniory of Staufen in Breisgau. ...About this time (ca. 1541) Faustus died in or not far from the town of Staufen in Breisgau. In his day he was as remarkable a sorcerer as could be found in German lands in our times. He had so many strange experiences at various times that he will not easily be forgotten for many years. He became an old man and, as it is said, died miserably. From all sorts of reports and conjectures many have thought that the evil spirit, whom in his lifetime he used to call his brother-in-law, had killed him. The books which he left behind fell into the hands of the count of Staufen, in whose territory he died. Afterwards many people tried to get these books and in doing so in my opinion were seeking a dangerous and unlucky treasure and gift. He sent a spirit into the monastery of the monks at Luxheim in the Vosges mountains – which they could not get rid of for years and which bothered them tremendously – and this for no other reason than that once upon a time they did not wish to put him up overnight. For this reason he sent them the restless guest.[1]

The details in this account contrast favorably with some of the brief, matter-of-fact presentations of most earlier sources. But as historical information, the content has, unfortunately, very little value. The original manuscript of the chronicle was written quite late (1564-6) about thirty years after the last reliable report of Faustus' activities. Here, as elsewhere in the chronicle, the authors display a strong interest in sensational story telling.[2] One suspects that their anecdotes concerning Faustus had gone through many hands. The incontestable fact that Faustus lived to be an old man seems to have survived the trials of time and retelling. It has not been possible to verify the death of Faustus in Staufen.[3] Nor has anyone succeeded in proving that Faustus had left behind a legacy of books. The date of Faustus' death is not given. There is only the vague association with the date of an event mentioned in the previous paragraph, the Regensburg Imperial Diet, which took place in 1541. To accept the validity of any part of this text seems precarious. The important role of the devil in the accounts indicates that the didactic element had taken over at the expense of historical facts. As in the table conversation of Luther, to be discussed later, Faustus supposedly called the devil his brother-in-law. The account of the *Zimmerische Chronik*, like the remarks of Luther, already demonstrate the evolution away from history and contribute primarily to the understanding of the early development of the Faustus legend.

Of more use in attempting to determine at least the approximate date of Faustus' death is a book published in 1539 by Philipp Begardi, a physician employed by the city of Worms, who had obtained his doctorate in medicine at the University of Mainz in 1518. In his *Index sanitatis*, which he wrote after twenty years of experience as a doctor,[4] he tries to expose the abuses and errors of doctors. In the chapter dealing with the topic of undesirable doctors, Begardi mentions Faustus.[5]

Immediately before writing about Faustus, Begardi speaks of Thessalus (a physician in the time of Emperor Nero) and Paracelsus, the well-known contemporary of Faustus. Begardi considers it particularly irritating and painful that the constant boasting of these men led them to throw all the former medical authorities overboard. He regrets that both arrogant men had a whole school of followers. From Thessalaus and Paracelsus, Begardi turns to Faustus, whom he considers somewhat different and yet still belonging to the same general group of undesirable practitioners of medicine.

> There is another well-known and important man whom I would not have mentioned were it not for the fact that he himself had no desire to remain in obscurity and unknown. For some years ago he traveled through almost all

countries, principalities and kingdoms, and himself made his name known to everybody and bragged much about his great skill not only in medicine but also in chiromancy, nigromancy, physiognomy, crystal gazing, and similar arts. And he not only bragged but confessed and signed himself as a famous experienced master. He himself avowed and did not deny that he was called Faustus and in addition signed himself "The philosopher of philosophers." The number of those who complained to me they were cheated by him was very great. Now his promises were great, like those of Thessalus; likewise his fame as that of Theophrastus. But his deeds, as I hear, were very petty and fraudulent. But in taking or – to speak more accurately – in receiving money he was not slow. And afterwards also, on his departure, as I have been informed, he left many to whistle for their money. But what is to be done about it? What's gone is gone. I will drop the subject here. Anything further is your affair.[6]

Begardi himself never met Faustus and had only secondhand information about him. Nevertheless, most of what he wrote appears credible. It seems plausible that those who complained to him about having been cheated also communicated generally reliable information. Residing in Worms, halfway between Heidelberg and Kreuznach, he lived in an area that Faustus must have traveled through more than once. Faustus' claim that he was the "philosopher of philosophers" is consistent with his academic background and his tendency to boast and to use hyperboles about himself. His claims to wisdom in many forms of divination and magic have been sufficiently demonstrated by other sources. Similarly, we are well acquainted with his ubiquitous nature. What Begardi wrote about Faustus is a logical extention, of the image presented by Trithemius and Mutianus. Therefore, there is no reason to doubt the implication of the concluding remark ("hin ist hin") that Faustus was no longer alive when Begardi wrote his book. The earlier reference to the time a few years before ("vor etlichen jaren") when Faustus had wandered all over the entire countryside supports this hypothesis. Since Begardi dedicated his book to the mayor of Worms on January 8, 1539, we many assume that Faustus died some time before 1539.

V

LUTHER AND THE NEW IMAGE OF FAUSTUS

> *Also auch, weil Zäuberei ein schändlicher, gräulicher Abfall ist, da einer sich von Gott, dem er gelobt und geschworen ist, zum Teufel, der Gottes Feind ist, begibt, so wird sie billig an Leib und Leben gestraft.*
>
> Luther, *Tischreden* ("Zäuberei auf theologisch abgemalet")

The influence of Martin Luther is the most important single factor in the development of the Faustus legend. At a very early point, within the lifetime of the historical Faustus, Luther made the first known pronouncements in which Faustus the magician was identified as a close associate of the devil, an association made in almost all of the anecdotes written after Faustus' death. Henceforth, the fate of Faustus was predictable. Once the association with the devil was established, later authors of anecdotes had a great deal of information and theological insight at their disposal to show the obvious implications of such sinful involvement.

No commentator on Faustus during the following five decades contributed to the legend as much as Luther did; nor did anyone offer information contradicting Luther's views. Nevertheless, before focusing on Luther as the major influence on the legend, two works, because of their wide circulation, deserve special attention.

In 1548 the Protestant pastor Johannes Gast wrote about Faustus in the second volume of his *Conviviales sermones*. This work was subsequently reprinted with volumes I and III in 1554 and 1566. Information about Faustus is given by Gast in two successive passages:

Concerning the Necromancer Faustus

He put up at night at a certain very rich monastery, intending to spend the night there. A brother placed before him some ordinary wine of indifferent quality and without flavor. Faustus requested that he draw from another cask a better wine, which it was the custom to give to nobles. Then the brother said: "I do not have the keys; the prior is sleeping, and it is a sin to awaken him." Faustus said: "The keys are lying in that corner. Take them and open that cask on the left and give me a drink." The brother objected that he had no orders from the prior to place any other wine before guests. "In a short time you shall see marvels, you inhospitable brother." Burning with rage, he left early in the morning without saying farewell and sent a certain raging devil who made a great stir in the monastery by day and by night and moved things about both in the church and in the cells of the monks, so that they could not get any rest, no matter what they did. Finally, they deliberated whether they should leave the monastery or destroy it altogether. And so they wrote to the Count of the Palatinate concerning the misfortune in which they were involved. He took the monastery under his own protection and ejected the monks to whom he furnishes supplies from year to year and uses what is left for himself. It is said that to this very day, if monks enter the monastery, such great disturbances arise that those who live there can have no peace. This the devil was able to bring to pass.

Another Story about Faustus

At Basel I dined with him in the great college and he gave to the cook various kinds of birds to roast. I do not know where he bought them or who gave them to him, since there were none for sale at the time. Moreover I never saw any like them in our regions. He had with him a dog and a horse which I believe to have been demons and which were ready for any service. I was told that the dog at times assumed the form of a servant and served the food. However the wretch was destined to come to a deplorable end, for he was strangled by the devil and this body on its bier kept turning face downward even though it was five times turned on its back. God preserve us lest we become slaves of the devil.[1]

Gast claims to have met Faustus personally, and this assertion has given his statements a strong appearance of authenticity. But a cautious approach is warranted, first of all, because the spirit of the devil, which did not appear in the primary sources, pervades Gast's anecdotes. The credibility of Gast is undermined, furthermore, by the very nature of his work. As the title indicates, it is a compilation of convivial discourses and stories, including jokes and witty sayings. The author is proud of his ability to present pleasant, useful as well as true stories, to be useful in after-dinner social situations. His choice of subjects included priests, peasants, landowners, kings, and emperors. Gast, who was a close associate of the reformers Oekolampad and Bullinger in Basel, showed his antipapal prejudice only in a few passages; clearly he hoped that Catholic readers might also find his book worthwhile. In the second volume, containing the passages about Faustus, the Protestant prejudice of the author is more evident than in the volume that had appeared seven years earlier. On the whole, Gast's expressed purpose to entertain as well as to be useful raises the question whether historical truth was an important consideration in reporting particular incidents.

Several passages in the *Sermones* correspond to material in Gast's diary. A comparison shows that Gast tended to expand and refine the original material for the sake of effect.[2] Often Gast's anecdotes can be shown to be based on third-hand information. Most critical, however, is Gast's questionable practice of telling anecdotes that he obviously derived from other sources in the first person.[3] For example, he reports that he personally participated in a dramatic escape incident during the Imperial Diet of 1529. The fact is, however, that the individual involved was not Gast but Melanchthon, as we learn from a commentary by Melanchthon on the prophet Daniel, printed in 1543.[4]

Therefore, we conclude that Gast's information about Faustus is highly unreliable as historical data. This is not to say that it is entirely fabricated. It is not necessary to doubt seriously that Faustus visited a monastery in which the monks then suffered some unpleasant consequences. Perhaps Gast had, in fact, met Faustus once. But the information that Faustus had sent a certain raging devil to haunt the monks was perhaps added to the story by the superstitious Gast or, more probably, by the person who related it to him.

It is interesting to note that Gast is not quite sure but suspects that the dog and horse belonging to Faustus were devils. This uncertainty appears to show that we are dealing with an early stage of the legend, just at the point at which apparently factual information first becomes considerably distorted by the force of assumptions. Was Gast perhaps influenced by the assumptions of others? Luther, for example, believed that the devil could hide in the form of almost any animal, including that of a dog.[5] There will be occasion to come back once more to the linking of Faustus' dog to the devil. At any rate, Gast also tells of the gruesome death of Faustus: "... strangled by the devil and his body kept turning face downward even though it was five times turned on its back." Once more we are confronted with the phenomenon of the legend making; it is clear that Gast, or his predecessor, was again taking recourse to certain assumptions about the consequences of dealing with the devil. In Luther's eyes, the manner in which the devil killed Faustus was similar to the way the devil had been killing many of his victims. It was Luther's belief that the devil strangled his victims and twisted their heads.[6]

A striking characteristic of Gast's anecdotes is that all elements depend on the idea of Faustus as a magician and close associate of the devil. Of course, Luther had presented this idea about fifteen years earlier. Although considerable physical distance as well as theological differences separated Wittenberg from Basel, Gast demonstrated an eager interest in literature by and about Luther.[7] We have just seen that Gast had not been shy about using Melanchthon as a source. It seems reasonable to suppose that Gast's Faustus anecdotes were not entirely original, having been subjected to Luther's influence before reaching him. This cannot be proved. But the following discussion of "Melanchthon's" anecdotes shows that the nature of Gast's reporting followed a pattern very similar to that which was characteristic of the stories originating in Luther's Wittenberg.

In 1562 Johannes Manlius published a collection of sayings or anecdotes that he based primarily on the lectures of his teacher at the University of Wittenberg, Philipp Melanchthon. This work has been discussed in connection with the evolution of the historical Georgius Faustus to the legendary Johannes Faustus.[8] The fact that all subsequent references to Faustus used the name Johannes exclusively offers strong evidence of the crucial role that this work played in the development of the legend. Similarly, this is the first time that Faustus' birthplace appears as Kundling instead of Helmstadt. Subsequent sources accepted this as reliable information, although it was found necessary by some to make a slight change to Knittlingen, the German equivalent of the name of Kundling. This brief "biography" by Melanchthon, edited by Manlius, represents the first and most comprehensive biographical information about Faustus. The book containing it was published in three different places with new editions in 1565, 1568, 1590, 1594, 1600, etc.; German editions in 1565, 1566, and 1574; excerpts published by Andreas Hondorf in 1568, 1570, 1571, 1572, 1573, 1574, 1575, 1577, 1582, 1583, 1584, 1585, 1595, 1597, etc.[9] Thus, we have here the most easily available as well as the most authoritative source on Faustus before the publication of the *Volksbuch* in 1587:

I knew a certain man by the name of Faustus from Kundling, which is a small town near my birthplace. When he was a student at Cracow he studied magic, for this art was much practiced in the city and in the university; he wandered about everywhere and talked of many mysterious things. When he wished to provide a spectacle at Venice, he said he would fly to heaven. So the devil raised him up and then cast him down so that he was dashed to the ground and almost killed. But he did not die.

A few years ago this same Johannes Faustus, on the day before his end, sat very downcast in a certain village in the Duchy of Württemberg. The innkeeper asked him why, contrary to his custom and habit, he was so downcast (he was otherwise a most shameful scoundrel, who led a very wicked life, so that he was again and again near to being killed because of his dissolute habits). Then he said to the innkeeper in the village: "Don't be frightened tonight." In the middle of the night the house was shaken. When Faustus did not get up in the morning, and when it was now almost noon, the innkeeper went with several others into his bedroom and found him lying near the bed with his face turned toward his back. The devil had killed him. While he was alive he had with him a dog, which was the devil, just as the scoundrel who wrote *De vanitate artium* likewise had a dog that ran about with him and was the devil. This same Faustus escaped from this town of Wittenberg when the good prince Duke Johannes had given orders to arrest him. Likewise, he escaped from Nuremberg. He was just beginning to dine when he became restless and immediately rose and paid the innkeeper what he owed. He hardly got outside the gate when the bailiffs came and inquired about him.

The same magus Faustus, a vile beast and a sewer of many devils, vainly boasted that all the victories that the imperial armies won in Italy had been gained through his magic. This was a malicious lie. I say this for the sake of the young people so that they do not instantly assent to such idle man.[10]

In specific passages Manlius relates information very closely related to Gast's. Both authors refer to Faustus' dog.

Gast:
Canem secum ducebat et equam, Satanas fuisse reor, qui ad omnia erant parati exequenda.

Melanchthon/Manlius:
Vivens, ad huc, habebat secum canem, qui erat diabolus, sicut iste nebulo qui scripsit De vanitate artium (i.e., Agrippa) etiam habebat canem, secum currentem, qui erat diabolus.

The story of Faustus' end is given in much greater detail by Manlius. The manner in which the devil kills his victim also has a familiar ring:

Gast:	Melanchthon/Manlius:
...a satana suffocatus, cuius cadauer in feretro facie ad terram perpetuo spectans, etsi quinquies in tergum uerteretur.	...hospes...invenitque eum iacentem prope lectum inversa facie, sic a diabolo interfectus.

There are many possible ways in which these similarities could have arisen. It is conceivable that either Melanchthon or Manlius had relied on Gast as a source and then expanded on the available material. On the other hand, it is possible that the "Melanchthon" stories evolved independently of Gast. Regardless of the solution to this question, the process involved is that of legend formation. It is a characteristic of the anecdotes of both Gast and Melanchthon/Manlius that they contribute little to an objective biography of Faustus. They reflect primarily beliefs about a magician who joins forces with the devil. Once a man has been made the friend of the devil he can be expected to be linked with traditional conceptions and stories associated with the devil. In these particular instances Gast and Melanchthon/Manlius were not relating historical facts but, rather, previously held beliefs. Melanchthon (or Manlius) believed that the well-known Agrippa von Nettesheim, a friend of Trithemius and a scholar of strong occult interests, had a dog that was, in fact, the devil. We have noted that Luther had also expressed the belief that devils could appear as dogs and that they killed their victims by twisting their heads. With these sources at least, beliefs about the devil had replaced historical facts as the main factor in the biographical writing about Faustus. Moreover, we are inclined to take the role of Luther much more seriously than scholars generally have done. At an early stage Luther had established the crucial connection between the magician Faustus and the devil, and this connection made the many later developments understandable, if not predictable.

Another aspect of this legend-formation comes to light as we compare the Melanchthon/Manlius text with the text of Melanchthon's lectures, on which they were based. The small mutation in the treatment of facts gives an indication of how vulnerable history was even in the hands of academic writers:

Melanchthon:	Melanchthon/Manlius
Ibi (coram Nerone) Simon Magus subuolare in coelum: sed Petrus precatus est vt decideret. Credo	Ille (Faustus) Venetiis cum vellet ostendere spectaculum, dixit se volaturum in coelum. Diabo-

Apostolos habuisse magna certami-
na, etiamsi non omnia sunt scripta.
Faustus Venetiis etiam hoc tentauit.
Sed male allisus solo.¹¹

lus igitur subvexit eum, et affli-
xit adeo, ut allisus humi pene
exanimatus esset: sed tamen non
est mortuus.

One additional reference to Faustus has been discovered in the lectures of Melanchthon. But Manlius related this incident as another example of magic, without mentioning the name of Faustus.

Melanchthon:
Diabolus est mirabilis artifex; potest enim aliqua arte efficere, quae nos non scimus. Denn er kan mehr, den die menschen konnen. Sicut narrantur multa magica prodigiosa, ut alias dixi de puella Bononiensi: Item Faustus magus deuoravit alium Magum Viennae, qui post paucos dies inuentus est in quodam specu. Der Teuffel kan viel wunderlichs dings: tamen ecclesia habet propria quaedam miracula.¹²

Melanchthon/Manlius:
Viennae fuerunt duo magi, quorum alter devoravit alterum: id est diabolus abduxit alterum in specum, in quo triduo latuit, deinde reversus est.

According to Manlius, Melanchthon "knew" Faustus ("Novi quendam nomine Faustum de Kundling, quod est parvum oppidum, patriae meae vicinum"). But what Melanchthon told his students about Faustus appears to contradict this assertion. Melanchthon certainly could not have seen Faustus in Venice or Vienna. The narration of the fantastic incidents that supposedly occurred there are infused with theological interpretation. The anecdote about Faustus' attempt to fly might seem credible if we did not have the story of Faustus eating up another magician. In this second anecdote it becomes clear that, like Johannes Gast and Martin Luther, Melanchthon assumed that Faustus had associated with the devil. Since the lectures in question were delivered between 1554 and 1557, Melanchthon was undoubtedly influenced by Luther's tendency to see in Faustus a magician and representative of the devil. Melanchthon had access to information about the historical Faustus because of his friendship with Joachim Camerarius and Johannes Virdung, but apparently his strongly superstitious nature and his interest in using the example of Faustus to make statements of theological significance made the historical figure unrecognizable. In the hands of Manlius the changing image of Faustus underwent even further mutations. His predecessors were motivated by theological ideals. He was guided by the resolve to present a smooth, entertaining, and consistent narrative. This is the obvious explanation of the additions he made to the sources available to him. What is brief and matter-of-fact in Melanchthon's lectures is drawn out with details that actually have no foundations in the sources. With regard to the incident in Venice, Manlius adds that Faustus had the desire to present a public spectacle and stated that he would fly. The devil then carried him into the air but (in throwing him down) almost killed him. In the Vienna story, Manlius adds that it was the devil who carried the other magician to a certain cave. The rediscovery of this magician, which is vaguely given as "a few days" in Melanchthon's lecture becomes very specific: three days. These additions may appear relatively minor. But they reflect with even more exaggerated emphasis the devil's role behind Faustus' magic. Manlius also transformed the tenor of Melanchthon's original discussion from an academic discussion to an entertaining narrative.

The way Manlius treats his sources makes us very skeptical of the historical value of the claims that contradict the facts given in the original sources. Did Manlius simply invent the name Johannes to make his biography more complete? Did he claim that Melanchthon knew Faustus and that Faustus came from a town near Melanchthon's birthplace (Bretten in Southwestern Germany) to make his story more convincing? Did he have Faustus study at the University of Cracow because this school was then famous for astronomy and astrology? Until now these questions have not been raised by scholars, and yet the possibility of affirmative answers to them forces one to rethink the role traditionally assigned to Manlius' Faustus biography, rejecting it as a source of information about the historical figure and focusing on its critical function as the most widespread narrative about the legendary Faustus before 1587.

After its publication in 1562 there is hardly a mention of Faustus which does not rely on Manlius' biography for information. The authority of Melanchthon's name and the assumption that the information was based on a personal acquaintance with Faustus had convinced contemporaries (as well as most scholars to the present time) that Manlius wrote about the historical Faustus. In fact, he was contributing to a development and general acceptance of a relatively new, legendary image that had begun with Luther's pronouncements on the subject, about thirty years earlier.

Thus, the anecdotes of Gast, Melanchthon, and Manlius show a clear trend. The assumption that Faustus was a magician in collusion with the devil and the tendency to develop new aspects of the legend on the basis of this assumption put the spotlight on Luther as the most likely source of these developments. A closer look at what he had to say about Faustus and the context of his pronouncements can certainly shed light on the origins of the legend.

Nicolaus Medler made the following record of a conversation Luther held sometime between October 24, 1533 and September 14, 1535:

> When one evening at the table a certain magician named Faustus was mentioned Doctor (Luther) said seriously: "The devil does not make use of the services of magicians against me, but if he had been able to harm me, he would have done it a long time ago. To be sure, he had me by the head, but he had to let me go. Yes, I have dealt with him, and at times, when he came with the Bible, he fixed it so that I hardly knew whether I was dead or alive; he made me despair so that I didn't know whether there was God, and he almost made me lose hope in God. In sum, there is no true refuge except directly in God himself; he can help you; for this just a single word is needed... [13]

Luther's reaction to Faustus reflects a total lack of interest in the objective reality: his concern was with the devil, not with Faustus. When Johannes Aurifaber edited and published this anecdote as one of the first pieces in his selection of *Tischreden* in 1566, he gave it the following title: "God's word alone conquers the burning darts and all temptations of the devil." One is reminded of the famous words of the Lutheran hymn:

> Und wenn die Welt voll Teufel wär
> Und wollt uns gar verschlingen...
> Ein Wörtlein kann ihn fällen.

By implication Luther condemns Faustus as the representative of the devil. Luther sees Faustus in the sinful, dark, and forbidden world of threatening spirits against whom the only recourse of man is God's word as revealed in the Bible, especially in the New Testament.

Consistent with this perspective, Luther treated the topic of Faustus again between June 18 und July 28, 1537. Luther's remarks were recorded by Antonius Lauterbach: "Mention was made of the conjurers and the art of magic and how Satan blinded men. Much was said about Faustus, who called the devil his brother-in-law, and the remark was made: 'If I, Martin Luther, had given him even my hand, he would have destroyed me, but I would not have been afraid of him; I would have given him my hand in the name of the Lord, with

God my protector. For I believe many magic tricks have been attempted against me.'"[14]

Again, magic and the devil are seen as one. Again, Luther demonstrates a total lack of interest in the personality of the magician, even though a lot of things were apparently said about it by others at Luther's table. For the reformer, Faustus the magician provided an occasion to remind people how dangerous magic was – the devil used it as a tool against men.

It is noteworthy that Antonius Lauterbach, who recorded Luther's remarks, referred to a very specific view held at this time about Faustus: that even Faustus himself "called the devil his brother-in-law." How did this idea originate? Our study of primary sources reveals nothing that would confirm this as a historical fact. Trithemius and the Nuremberg authorities condemned Faustus and saw him dealing with forbidden arts, but in their critical statements they stopped short of references to the devil. Luther was clearly the first most influential proponent of the connection between Faustus and the devil. Without him this connection might not have become the primary catalyst of the legend.

But Luther's significance for the fate of the legend is not to be measured simply by the influence exerted by the two conversations mentioned. The views he expressed in these conversations were very similar to those which he expressed over and over in other contexts. The conception of the magician as an associate of the devil was an essential part of the Reformation ideology that reshaped religious thought in Germany during the sixteenth century.

Luther's image of the devil and the devil's significant relationship to magic had their origins in early childhood experiences. The strong superstitions of the parents undoubtedly made an indelible mark on the young Luther. We learn from Luther that his mother used to be tormented by a witch *(Zauberin)* in the neighborhood and was forced to appease her. This witch also frightened the children with her tricks and was responsible for the death of a preacher who had spoken out against her.[15] Luther relates another anecdote that shows his father to have been similarly plagued by anxieties about the devil's doings. Luther's father had been called to the bedside of a deathly ill neighbor. The dying man pointed to his posterior and said: "Look dear Luther, and see how they (the devils) have lashed me!" This experience frightened the older Luther so much that he himself almost died.[16] Martin Luther also recalled that the mines were especially densely populated with devils who deluded the miners (of whom his father was one) in their search for metal. The father's tendency to immediately see the devil's work in any unpleasant phenomenon can be recognized also when he showed his anger about Luther's entry into a monastery. About this decision he exclaimed: "God give that it wasn't a devil's spook *(Satanae praestigium).*"[17] It was Luther's belief that witches (whom he put in the same class as magicians) were much more numerous in the time of his childhood, before the Reformation and his new revelations about the Bible.[18] They were, at any rate, a source of great anxiety to the young Luther who even attributed the death of one of his brothers to the magical power and influence of a witch.[19]

An awareness of these early experiences makes it easier to visualize the development of Luther's attitude to magic and magicians. Later views and teachings show that this development was not an isolated incident, but part and parcel of the new Lutheran ideology. The Bible, Luther's prime source of authority, only confirmed the Reformer's fears of magic and the reality of the devil. In this connection St. Paul and the Book of Job in particular gave him inspiration and guidance.[20] In the mature Luther's writings the characteristics ascribed to the devil and the magician are very similar. Both are powerful; both suffer from excessive pride; both rebel against God; and both achieve their ends by deluding their victims.[21] For those who subscribed to Luther's views, it must have appeared that anything true about the devil had to apply with equal validity to the magician, hence to Faustus as well. This approach certainly encouraged liberties with the historical sources. It might serve as a plausible explanation for the liberties actually observed in the formation of the Faustus legend.

Luther did not write a biography of Faustus. But in a sense he came very close to it. There is hardly a passage in the 1587 *Volksbuch* that cannot be related directly to a closely corresponding passage in Luther's works. Whenever Luther wrote about magicians or the devil, he appeared to foreshadow the details and general tenor of the legend. There is, of course, the list of anecdotes that were taken from Luther's works directly. For example, during his conversation about Faustus in 1537 Luther told three anecdotes about magic and the power of the devil to delude the senses; about a man who devoured a peasant together with horse and wagon, about a monk who ate more than half a wagon of hay, and about a debtor who allowed his creditor, a Jew, to pull out one of his legs. These anecdotes were expanded, identified with Faustus, and included in the other stories of the *Volksbuch*. The same fate befell stories Luther told elsewhere about the Emperor, Frederick III, the Abbot of Sponheim (i.e., Trithemius), and the devil's attacks upon a pious old man.[22] A study of the origins and transformations of these stories would in itself deserve a book-length study.

More significant perhaps than the general agreement of anecdotes about magicians is the crucial idea of a pact with the devil, since Luther believed that every magician made such a pact.[23] In this pact Luther saw the secret behind all magical power and accomplishments. One story Luther told may be considered exemplary and can be taken to illustrate the manner in which Luther foreshadowed the most significant aspects of the later image of Faustus:

> In Erfurt they burned a soothsayer and practitioner of black magic. For a number of years he had been very sad because of his great poverty. Then he came upon the devil himself, who promised him great things, that he would be rich if he were to reject baptism and salvation through Christ and to deny the will ever to do penance. The poor man accepted these conditions, and the devil then gave him a crystal ball from which he could tell the future and thereby receive fame and riches. Finally, the devil really deceived him and showed his true character by having him accuse innocent people of theft on the basis of his crystal ball. Because of this he was thrown into prison. He revealed then that he broke the pact he had made with the devil, and he asked for a pastor. He performed penance, and his example put the fear of God in many people. He died with a joyful heart, in spite of his punishment. Thus, the devil was beaten at his own game, and his evil intentions were made evident.[24]

One is reminded of the Theophilus legend, in which the ending appears positive in spite of the seriousness of the pact. In general, however, Luther believed that signing a pact with the devil was such a grave sin that it certainly brought with it the triumph of hell and the eternal death of the soul. In fact, Luther approved of this kind of drastic ending.

Goethe complained once very bitterly about Luther for populating the entire visible world with the devil and for making this world a personification of the devil.[25] Luther's conception of the devil was a unique and significant aspect of his view of the world. It was a phenomenon that could not be isolated from the progress of the entire Reformation movement. It was strongly reflected in the literature of the time, aside from the story of Faustus.[26] Even if later writers were unacquainted with Luther's specific pronouncements on Faustus, they could not avoid his influence. Inspiration for the ever increasing role of the devil in the Faustus legend could have come, directly or indirectly, from countless passages in Luther's works, sermons, lectures, or conversations. It is only natural that Gast, Melanchthon, and Manlius, who were clearly well acquainted with Luther's thought, should have been the ones to take up the topic of Faustus and to add to it in a spirit consistent with Luther's ideology. The legend moved thus with the momentum of the Reformation as if on the crest of a wave. The force of its movement covered up without difficulty the historical facts, from which it originated, reacted to, and, in many respects, contradicted.

VI

THE METAMORPHOSIS OF FAUSTUS

> *Ich gebe dem Atlas auch einen Plan bei...*
> *Wenn man sich aber bei Ansicht dieses Plans in seinen Erwartungen getäuscht sieht und findet, daß Troja für die großen Taten der Ilias viel zu klein war und Homer alles mit dichterischer Freiheit übertrieben hat, so muß man doch andererseits eine hohe Genugtuung in der nunmehr erlangten Gewißheit finden, daß es wirklich Troja gab, daß Troja aufgedeckt ist und daß den Homerischen Gesängen wirkliche Tatsachen zu Grunde liegen.*
>
> Heinrich Schliemann, *Ausgrabungen in Troja* (1873)

Sometime between the end of his studies at Heidelberg in 1487 and the occasion of his encounter with Trithemius in 1507 Georg Helmstetter adopted the name Faustus, which he retained throughout his life. The many versions of the legend in the sixteenth century generally referred to him also as Faustus. In 1565, the first translation of Manlius' *Collectanea* used the form Faust, but this mistaken "translation" of the Latin name into a German one was corrected in subsequent editions. Marlowe's drama, written towards the end of the century, referred to Doctor Faustus. In the seventeenth century the number of references to Faust, rather than Faustus, increased. For example, Grimmelshausen's *Simplicissimus* (chapter 18) refers to Faust. It was not until after the publication of Goethe's *Faust*, however, that the name of Faustus became generally transformed into Faust in fictional as well as historical literature.

The name Faust represents a very late manifestation of the legend formation under Goethe's influence. The name Faustus reflects more accurately the conscious identification of the historical figure with a humanistic practice and indicates Faustus' strong concern about reputation.

The transformation of the historical name Georgius into the legendary

Johannes occurred in printed sources for the first time in 1562 in *Collectanea*. One can now only speculate about the reasons for this change. But it is a fact that the sources between 1528 and 1562 refer simply to Faustus. It is therefore conceivable that the name Johannes was an educated guess on the part of Manlius. The name Manlius used was the most common first name and happened to be, by a characteristic coincidence, identical with his own first name.

Manlius was also the first to publish information contradicting the fact that Faustus hailed from Helmstadt, about twenty kilometers from Heidelberg. According to Manlius' report Faustus came from the village of Kundling, near Melanchthon's birthplace. On the basis of the questionable authority of Manlius, Kundling has been understood to refer to Knittlingen, where a museum today still celebrates the memory of the "historical Faust." The author of the 1587 *Volksbuch* brought about a further mutation when he claimed that Faustus had been born in Rod(a) near Weimar. Information about what and where Faustus had studied underwent analogous mutations: The historical Faustus had studied philosophy at Heidelberg. According to Manlius' report, he studied magic at Cracow. But the university records there do not confirm this assertion. Finally, in the *Volksbuch* we find him graduating as a doctor of theology at the University of Wittenberg. In general, the philosopher Faustus, who wandered about chiefly in Southern Germany, and whose patrons were Catholics, gradually became a renegade theologian and alumnus of the foremost university of the Reformation movement. This shift from south to north, from philosophy to theology, and from Catholic to Protestant runs parallel to the increasing role played by the Wittenberg theologians Luther and Melanchthon. These critics of Faustus apparently preferred to treat their subject in a context and geographical area most familiar to them.

Faustus was particularly proud of his extensive academic background in philosophy. He appears to have earned his living primarily as an astrologer. But he also claimed competency as a magician, and the authors of the legend reacted most strongly to this particular occupation. They tended to neglect Faustus as philosopher and astrologer, the roles that helped the historical figure attain a certain degree of respectability.

Faustus was a philosopher without really being dedicated to academic life; he gave the appearance of having humanistic ideals without hiding his primary interest in monetary gain. Although there is evidence that at least some of his predictions were accurate, the extreme audacity of his claims and behavior suggests that he probably experienced many failures as well.

The historical Faustus was accused of sexual perversion. One source implies that he was a homosexual; another labels him a sodomite. If one could be certain, there would be additional evidence for his extraordinary audacity. But we have reason to be skeptical about the reliability of available information. Accusations of promiscuity were commonly leveled against persons who, like Faustus, held unorthodox views. The early anecdotes do not treat this subject. The author of the *Volksbuch* also takes up the topic of sexual behavior, and he depicts, with obvious pleasure, the adventures of Faustus in a Turkish harem and Faustus' experiences with beautiful women of many nationalities, including Helen of Troy. Some of the women the devil procured for Faustus were actually demons. These stories of sexual adventures in the *Volksbuch* were obviously fabricated, based perhaps on fantasies about witches or on associations inherited from the Middle Ages, according to which unorthodox beliefs and immoral sexual behavior went hand in hand. The reputation of the historical Faustus may have suffered from the power of similar fantasies and associations.

The historical Faustus had a strongly ambivalent character. Some saw him as a genuine philosopher; others considered him a charlatan. Mutianus Rufus related that the boastings of Faustus held many people spellbound. On the other hand, the city of Ingolstadt was unhappy about his activities as a soothsayer and expelled him. Despite these detractions, he was able to win significant patrons: Franz von Sickingen, Daniel Stibar, Philipp von Hutten, and the Bishop of Bamberg. The list of his critics is equally impressive: Johannes Trithemius, Mutianus Rufus, Kilian Leib, and Joachim Camerarius.

The image of the historical Faustus mirrors the prevalent diversity of beliefs, doubts, and superstitions about the occult. In contrast, the advent of the legend marked the gradual disappearance of ambivalence in the image of Faustus. The authors of the legend were persistent in portraying a powerful magician who had the help of the devil. They did not dwell on traits that might distract the reader from this main theme.

If the legendary Faustus was condemned for his curiosity in the forbidden occult sciences, many contemporaries and even critics of the historical figure deserved a similarly severe judgment. The natural magic of Trithemius and the humanistic divination of Camerarius reflected an intense involvement in the occult. By attributing to Faustus an anecdote originally related about Trithemius, the author of the *Volksbuch* condemned, by implication, not just Faustus but a whole generation that looked with curiosity and benevolence to a renaissance in the occult sciences.

The audacity of the historical Faustus, most dramatically manifest in Trithemius' letter, was the one personality trait that remained closely linked with Faustus' name even in most legendary accounts of his life. This boldness is closely related to his conscious self-advertising. It appears that he himself gave a powerful impetus to the evolution of his legend. His calling card shows that he wished to be known as the heroic successor and representative of former great magicians. This kind of boasting bordered, however, on recklessness, for Faustus claimed wisdom in arts that many considered to be black magic.

In the primary sources, Faustus is never referred to as an associate of the devil. There is no evidence that he ever claimed to be the devil's brother-in-law. But he did consider himself to be the ultimate authority on necromancy, an occult practice that, according to Trithemius, at least, involved a pact with the devil. This kind of recklessness might have been responsible for the hostile and slanderous reference to Faustus as *nigromanticus* (practitioner of black magic) by the Nuremberg authorities in 1532. Then Luther, within less than three years, saw Faustus as a magician in league with the devil. If Faustus had demonstrated a degree of modesty or moderation, he might have prevented this development.

It has been suggested that the historical Fausts was inspired by the heretical doctrines of gnosticism.[1] But available historical evidence does not support these assertions. This is not to say that the activities of Faustus, who called himself "magus secundus" and thus recognized the primacy of Zoroaster, did not appear reminiscent of Simon Magus, the much maligned representative of gnosticism in Christian literature. Thus, at an early stage in the legend Melanchthon linked the devil-inspired magic of Faustus and Simon Magus. The historical Faustus, bold as he was, seems to have stopped short of making such a dangerous identification.

The contemporary sources do not reveal when and how Faustus died, while, on the other hand, numerous later sources describe in gruesome detail his violent death at the hands of the devil. These later sources share elements that were probably inspired by Luther's ideas about how the devil killed his victims. It seems, therefore, that Luther's influence, which was responsible for focusing on the sinful alliance between Faustus and the devil, was also responsible for suggesting the appropriate punishment.

In general, the evolution of the Faustus legend does not appear to be an arbitrary process. It has been observed that stories such as the one about Faustus were not the products of the imagination but represented logical and necessary exaggerations of the facts.² Our study shows that exaggerations, additions, and omissions were at the root of the many mutations. At almost every point the character of the primary sources as well as of the far-fetched anecdotes was affected by a strong subjective element; those who wrote about Faustus also imposed their own beliefs and, unconsciously, revealed the dominating ideology of their time. It is important to keep in mind that the sixteenth century saw historical or factual truth in a less sophisticated way than does the present time. In the Renaissance and Reformation era moral teachings represented a higher form of truth than factual truth.³ It is not surprising that moral and theological interpretations made the survival of historical facts precarious. At a very early stage the sublime, moral truth of the theologians took the place of factual truth in the stories about Faustus.

The infusion of moral truth may be noted in the earliest reactions to Faustus. But these early reactions were not dictated by a common ideology; they were characterized primarily by their diversity. Faustus' contemporaries were willing to concede that an academic approach to divination and magic was not necessarily sinful. Faustus, no less than his contemporaries Trithemius and Camerarius, contributed to and profited from this liberal attitude. Diverse occult practices like magic and astrology for monetary gain, mystical natural magic, and idealistic astrological politics existed side by side and thrived in spite of criticism.

The age that created and popularized the Faustus legend was far less tolerant. The authors and propagators of the legend – haunted by the fear of an onmipresent devil – were no longer willing or able to distinguish between academic and nonacademic magic, between natural and black magic, and even between educated magicians and uneducated witches.⁴ Trithemius, Agrippa, and Faustus were equally maligned and persecuted in anecdotes written during this later period. Fantasies about devil pacts, promiscuity, and magical activities (for example, flying), generally marshalled to accuse witches, were also fanatically applied to these practitioners of Renaissance magic.

The legend about Faustus' pact with the devil and subsequent punishment in hell was written in the age of the European witch craze. It was an age when Catholics competed with Protestants in hunting and exterminating women who presumably practiced some form of demonic magic.⁵ We have seen that in the 1560s the legend of Faustus, the story of the "devil's brother-in-law," began to flourish. This same period experienced the beginnings of unprecedented witch hunts and burnings.⁶ When the *Volksbuch* appeared in 1587, the phenomenal popularity of the legendary Faustus was matched by a high point in the intensity of witch burnings in Germany.[7] This extraordinary historical coincidence makes the notoriety as well as popularity of the legendary Faustus plausible.

A common ideology is characteristic of later reactions to Faustus. This ideology recognized no redeeming qualities in magicians. The practice of magic implied a pact with the devil and invited eternal punishment. As far as we can tell, Luther was the first to judge Faustus in this manner. Thus, he established the more sublime, moral truth of the legend, and it was now only a question of time before a new generation, guided primarily by the reformer's thought, rejected and suppressed the tolerant Renaissance views about the magician Faustus.

In general, the legend acquired features of a polemic against the historical Faustus and the age he represented. The surviving stories were organized according to a new principle and infused with the subjective imprint of a new generation. Additions to and deletions from these stories were logical and necessary in order to eliminate the apparent inconsistencies in the "historical" anecdotes in favor of a more sublime as well as a more entertaining narrative. Ironically, this process, which entailed the destruction of historical facts and the superimposition of the polemical spirit of one age over the tolerance of an earlier one, was apparently necessary also to transform the image of the historical Faustus into an inspiring subject of modern European literature. The recovery of the historical Faustus, underneath numerous layers of fiction, enables us to understand his unique metamorphosis.

NOTES – INTRODUCTION

¹ "Es gibt keine zusammenhängende Lebensbeschreibung des historischen Faust. Das Bild, das wir von ihm haben, ist ein buntes Mosaik, zusammengeflickt aus gelegentlichen und sich stark widersprechenden Äußerungen seiner Zeitgenossen – und auch da bereits verschmelzen häufig Sage und Wirklichkeit." Hermann Reske, *Faust. Eine Einführung* (Stuttgart: Kohlhammer, 1971), p. 10.
² Hans Henning, *Faust-Bibliographie* (Berlin: Aufbau, 1966), I, 87-105.
³ "Daß in der Blütezeit der Hexenprozesse gegen Ende des 16. und während des 17. Jahrhunderts, Katholischen und Protestanten in der Verfolgung der Hexen miteinander wetteiferten, wird heute allgemein anerkannt." Nicolaus Paulus, *Hexenwahn und Hexenprozeß vornehmlich im 16. Jahrhundert* (Freiburg: Herder, 1910), p. 67. The Don Juan legend, which has much in common with the legend of Faustus, originated in Catholic territories. Evidence that the story of Faustus might have gone in a similar direction is the recently discovered reference to Faustus in the *Annales ecclesiastici* (Rome, 1646-77), a history of the church begun by Baronius and continued by Odorico Rinaldi. Rinaldi describes Faustus as a forerunner of Luther. He based his knowledge of Faustus on information supplied by Johannes Trithemius. Karl P. Wentersdorf, "A Faust-Splitter from Rome," *Seminar* 10 (1974), pp. 101-3.
⁴ A number of Henning's conclusions are based on insufficient evidence and will be disproved in the course of this study: "...ein akademischer Grad Fausts (muß) als angemaßt betrachtet werden.../ Die Berechtigung der Faust-Gedenkstätte im (Knittlinger) Rathaus kann somit anerkannt werden. / ...die Möglichkeit besteht, daß das eine oder andere noch unbekannte Zeugnis über Fausts Leben entdeckt, uns bekannte ergänzt werden oder in anderem Lichte erscheinen können. Doch ist kaum mit einem grundsätzlichen Wandel unserer Kenntnisse zu rechnen. / Mit der Abfassung des Faust-Buches von 1587 tritt eine erneute Verwandlung der Gestalt Fausts ein. Durch reformatorische Einflüsse wird aus dem so überaus lebendig gebliebenen Faust ein abschreckendes Bild des dem Teufel verfallenen Menschen." Hans Henning, "Faust als historische Gestalt," *Jahrbuch der Goethe-Gesellschaft*, 21 (1959), 107-39.
⁵ Ernst Meyer, *Heinrich Schliemann. Kaufmann und Forscher* (Göttingen: Musterschmidt, 1969), p. 275.

Notes – I. Who was Faustus?

¹ Will-Erich Peuckert, "Dr. Johannes Faust," *Zeitschrift für deutsche Philologie*, 70 (1947), 55-74.
² Hans Henning, "Faust als historische Gestalt," pp. 108-25. Alfred Zastrau writes "*Faust* (Doctor Faust, Sabellicus), Johannes (Georg), geb. 1480 Knittlingen b. Maulbronn (Württemberg), gest. 1540/1 Staufen (Breisgau)." "Faust," *Neue Deutsche Biographie*, V, 34-5.
³ The full title of Manlius' book indicates how it came into being: *Locorum communium collectanea*

a Iohanne Manlio per multos annos pleraque tum ex Lectionibus D. Philippi Melanchthonis, tum ex aliorum doctissimorum virorum relationibus excerpta, et nuper in ordinem ab eodem redacta (Basel: J. Oporinus, 1562). Faustus is treated on pp. 42-44 Cf. Wilhelm Meyer, "Nürnberger Faustgeschichten," *Abhandlungen der philosophisch-philologischen Klasse der königlichen Bayerischen Akademie der Wissenschaften*, 20 (1897), 340. Caspar Peucer, Melanchthon's son-in-law, complained that Manlius was extremely inaccurate in editing Melanchthon's works. Cf. Friedrich Wilhelm Bierling (in a chapter on the historical Faustus), *Commentatio de Pyrrhonismo historico* (Leipzig: N. Foester, 1724), p. 162. A very similar opinion was expressed by Joachim Camerarius in *De Philippi Melanchthonis ortu, totius vitae curriculo, et morte* (Leipzig: E. Vogel, 1566), p. 88. On the basis of Manlius' statement "Novi quendam nomina Faustum de Kundling" it has been assumed that Faustus had been born in Knittlingen. Cf. Matthias Simon, "Johannes Manlius, der erste Herausgeber von Melanchthonbriefen," *Zeitschrift für Bayerische Kirchengeschichte*, 24 (1955), 141-9. But the information supplied by Melanchthon in his lectures does not inspire faith either. P.M. Palmer and R.P. More, *The Sources of the Faust Tradition from Simon Magus to Lessing* (New York: Oxford Univ. Press, 1936). Further references by Melanchthon to Faustus cited in Gustav Milschack, *Gesammelte Aufsätze* (Wolfenbüttel, 1922), Col. 234.
[4] Karl Hartfelder, "Der Aberglaube Philipp Melanchthons," *Historisches Taschenbuch*, 6 (1889), 233-69.
[5] Città del Vaticano, Cod. Pal. lat. 730, fol. 174^v.
[6] Frankfurt, Stadt- und Universitätsbibliothek, Cod. lat. oct. 8, fol. 97^r.
[7] Staatsarchiv Bamberg, "Hofkammerrechnungen des Kreisarchivs Bamberg, pro diversis." (H 231, N. 1741).
[8] Stadtarchiv Ingolstadt, "Ingolstädter Ratsprotokollen, Verwiesen."
[9] Bayerische Staatsbibliothek München, 4° L impr. c. n. mss. 73, fol. 257^r.
[10] Stadtarchiv Nürnberg, "Ratsverlässe," Nr. 870, fol. 12^r.
[11] Joachim Camerarius, *Libellus Novus* (Leipzig: J. Rhomba, 1568), fol. X^r. The difficult question of the reliability of the testimony of Camerarius and Hutten requires, of course, further discussion. A thorough treatment of this problem is essential for the biographical study of Faustus. Briefly, it should be noted that the letters of Camerarius and Hutten have been preserved only in the context of later printed materials. But since the accuracy of the information supplied in these letters is confirmed by other contemporary documents, there is no need to doubt their reliability. Cf. chapter III (Camerarius).
[12] *Historisch-Literarisches Magazin*, ed. J. G. Meusel, 1 (1785), 93. Unfortunately, Meusel neglected to give the precise location of his manuscript. The authenticity of the letters printed here is confirmed by the fact that identical excerpts are found printed independently in Fernando Cortes, *Von dem Newen Hispanien* (Augsburg: B. Ulhart, 1550), fol. 51-60^r.
[13] Henning himself treats these sources with a certain degree of skepticism: the Maulbronn register of abbots (written down in the eighteenth century!); Agrippa von Nettenheim's letter about a German magician without reference to the name of Faustus; the papal legate Minucci referring to Faustus in 1583; Johannes Wier's *De praestigiis Daemonum* on Faustus (1568); Christoph Rosshirt's Nuremberg stories (ca. 1570); Zacharias Hogel's stories of Faustus in Erfurt (1650); etc. H. Henning, "Faust als historische Gestalt," pp. 120-34.
[14] K. A. von Reichlin-Meldegg, "Die deutschen Volksbücher von Faust und Wagner," *Kloster* (Stuttgart, 1849), pp. 11 and 330-1. Henning, "Faust als historische Gestalt," pp. 112-4. Palmer and More, pp. 86-7.
[15] A very famous Italian historian of this time was known by the name Sabellicus. This name was also an adopted one, chosen to indicate the historian's birthplace. "Sabellicus (March-Antoine), historien italien, naquit en 1436, à Vicovaro, dans la campagne de Rome, sur les confins de

l'ancien pays the Sabins; ce qui lui fit substituer a son nom de Coccio celui de Cocceius Sabellicus. Il était élève de Pomponius Laetus, et fut appelé, en 1475, à Udine, comme professeur d'éloquence...Il mourut à Venise...en 1508." *Biographie Universelle* (Paris, 1825), vol. 39, p. 434. Sabellicus' teacher, Pomponius Laetus, was the most famous early propagator of the idea that humanists should adopt Latin names. Therefore, it is significant that the most famous Faustus of this time, Publius Faustus Andrelinus, professor of rhetoric in Paris, had been similarly a student of Pomponius Laetus. This coincidence suggests that the German Faustus was, directly or indirectly, under the influence of the new humanistic tradition of adopting names, just as his contemporary Conrad Celtis. (Cf. chap. III, note 36) There are many accounts which confirm the popular belief that the land of the Sabines, even at this time, had a very special relationship to the occult. Cf. Jacob Burckhardt, *The Civilization of the Renaissance in Italy* (New York: Harper, 1958), II, pp. 500-1. Goethe treats this topic in a lengthy footnote to his translation of Benvenuto Cellini's autobiography. *Leben des Benvenuto Cellini von ihm selbst geschrieben, übersetzt und mit einem Anhang herausgegeben von Goethe* (Hamburg: Rowohlt, 1967), pp. 85-88 and 328. Moreover, it is reasonable to suppose that Faustus Andrelinus inspired the name that first appears as "Faustus iunior." Gustav Schwetschke, "Wer war Faustus senior? Ein Beitrag zur Faustgeschichte," *Deutsches Museum*, Oct. 11, 1855, pp. 548-51. Andrelinus lectured also on astronomy and wrote a book entitled *De influentia siderum et querela Parisiensis pavimenti* (Paris, 1497).

[16] Martin Luther, *Werke. Briefwechsel* (Weimar: Böhlau, 1930), I, 118-9.

[17] Kurt Scheinert, "Neue Faustsplitter," in *Beiträge zur deutschen und nordischen Literatur. Festgabe für Leopold Magon*, ed. by Hans Werner Seiffert (Berlin, 1958), pp. 72-4.

[18] Until recently biographers of Cusanus were unaware of the fact that Cusanus, as Nicolaus Treverensis, had been the discoverer of the lost plays of Plautus. Frank Baron, "Plautus und die deutschen Frühhumanisten," *Studia humanitatis. Ernesto Grassi zum 70. Geburtstag.* Hrsg. von E. Hora und E. Kessler (München: Fink, 1973), p. 90. On Celtis (Conradus Celtis de Epipoli *(sic)* and Conradus Bickel de Wyttfeld) see Gustav Toepke, *Die Matrikel der Universität Heidelberg* (Heidelberg, 1884-1893), I, p. 377 and II, pp. 415-6. "Es war ziemlich verbreitete Sitte damaliger Gelehrten, statt eines unbekannten Dörfchens die nächstliegende Stadt, namentlich wenn sie zugleich der Ort der Schulbildung war, als Geburtsort zu bezeichnen." Carl Krause, *Helius Eobanus Hessus. Sein Leben und seine Werke* (Gotha, 1879, repr. Nieuwkoop: B. de Graaf, 1963), I, p. 5.

[19] The original letter of Mutianus Rufus was copied by Heinrich Urban, to whom it was addressed. A careful examination of the manuscript indicates that the corrupted form Helmithius could have arisen because Urban was unable to decipher the letter at this point. In Urban's handwriting the difference between the letters i and s is a matter of length, and therefore one may even suspect that he was actually approximating an s as it appeared in the original letter (i.e., Helmstheus). This is essentially Schottenloher's explanation: "Von Konrad Mutianus, einem berühmten Zeitgenossen, wird Faust einmal "Helmitheus Hedelbergensis" genannt. Die Stelle, die schon viel Kopfzerbrechen verursacht hat, ist ohne Zweifel falsch überliefert: der Brief, in dem sie steht, ist leider nur in einer fehlerhaften Abschrift erhalten. Durch die Angabe Leibs dürfte nun der Weg zur richtigen Erklärung gefunden sein. Man schreibe das Wort "Helmitheus" und die Abkürzung "Helmsteten(sis) lateinisch untereinander, und man wird die falsche Leseart sofort erkennen. Und für den Zusatz "Hedelbergensis" hat mir Herr Geheimrat v. Riezler freundlichst den richtigen Weg gewiesen. Unter Helmstadt wird nämlich der Stammsitz der Grafen von Helmstadt, ein kleiner Ort im Bezirk Sinsheim, gemeint sein, der nicht weit von Heidelberg liegt. Die rätselhafte Bezeichnung "Faustus Helmitheus Hedelbergensis" wäre also nicht anders als "Faust *(sic)* von Helmstadt im Heidelbergischen" zu deuten." *Münchener neuste Nachrichten,* July 5, 1913 (no. 338). Als in Franz Babinger, "Der geschichtliche Faust," *Alemannia*. 41. (1914), 153.

Ernst Beutler states: "Urban hat die Abkürzung Helmstadt nicht auflösen können, da er natürlich eine Doppelung des Ortsnamen nicht erwartete." Ernst Beutler, "Georg Faust aus Helmstadt," *Goethe-Kalender* (1936), 184.

[20] "Die Titel Magister und Doktor hatten gleiche Bedeutung; nur war es üblich geworden, in den oberen Fakultäten regelmäßig Doktor zu gebrauchen, bei den Artisten dagegen Magister... Allein es begegnet doch auch, z.B. in den Wiener Statuten, für die Juristen der Titel Magister, statt Doktor und umgekehrt für die Artisten der Titel Doktor statt Magister." Georg Kaufmann, *Geschichte der deutschen Universitäten* (Stuttgart, 1888), II, pp. 274-5. Johannes Trithemius referred to his brother, who had a master's degree, as "artium et philosophiae doctor." Città del Vaticano, Cod. Pal. lat. 730, f. 2v and 190r.

[21] Karl Schottenloher was the first to make the identification. But he reported his find in a newspaper (cf. footnote no. 19), and references to the studies of Faustus in Heidelberg have not been registered in serious scholarly articles. Cf. Karl Hoffmann, "Heimat und Name des geschichtlichen Dr. Faust. War es Georg Helmstetter aus Heidelberg?" *550 Jahre Universität Heidelberg. Sonderbeilage der Heidelberger Neusten Nachrichten*, June 27, 1936, pp. 11-2.

[22] I am grateful to Dr. Weisert of the University of Heidelberg Archives for supplying me with references to Helmstetter from the manuscripts of the Faculty of Arts. I am also indebted to Professor Hans Eggers for giving me the following information on the various forms of the name Georg: "In lateinischen Namen auf -ius wie hier Georgius setzt sich in der gallo-romanischen Vulgärsprache anstelle des Nominativs die Endung -o (lat. Dativ) durch. [Vgl. G. Rohlfs, *Vom Vulgärlatein zum Altfranzösischen* (Tübingen, 1960), S. 30 f.]. Der laut g entwickelt sich im Galloromanischen vor e und i zu dj, was in der Schreibung oft nicht berücksichtigt wird [vgl. E. Richter, "Beiträge zur Geschichte der Romanismen," *Beihefte zur Zeitschrift für Romanische Philologie* (1934), S. 72 f.]. Die Hiatusgruppe e-o verliert in einigen romanischen Dialekten das unbetonte e (vgl. Richter, S. 49 f.). Das Endergebnis sind im Gallo-romanischen Namensformen wie Jorius, Jorio. Sie müssen ähnlich ausgesprochen worden sein, wie heute noch das englische George. In der Form Jorio geht der Name aus dem Gallo-romanischen in das Altdeutsche über. Belege dafür gibt es bereits im 8. Jahrhundert. Im späteren Mittelalter lassen sich 2 Formen unterscheiden, eine süddeutsche, die Georius, Georio oder ähnlich geschrieben wird, und eine fränkisch-rheinische Jorius, Jorg, Jörg u.a. Heidelberg liegt natürlich im rheinischen Dialektgebiet und eine Schreibung des Namens mit einem j am Anfang und Auslassung des zweiten entspricht daher auch im 14. und 15. Jahrhundert durchaus der dort gesprochenen Mundart."

Notes – II. At the University of Heidelberg

[1] "Georius Helmstetter dioc. Wormaciensis nona January" (1483), Toepke, *Matrikel*, I, p. 370.

[2] "Anno vero supra (1484) die ultima mensis Junii, congregatione magistrorum de facultate arcium facta omnes defectus baccalaureandorum delati sunt ad aures praefate facultatis arcium et discussi et cum Jorio de Helmstat, qui defectus temporis et alios habuit, dispensatum fuit, quod haberet magistrum pro eo deponentem iuxta statutum predicti facultatis, pro que et magister Johannes Hasse deposuit, prestito corporali iuramento coram facultate, et pro Johanne de Gretzingen idem magister Johannes Hasse modo quo supra coram magistris temptatoribus." UAH I, 3, No. 49, fol. 113v (Akten der Artistenfakultät, vol. 2, 1445-1501).

[3] "Anno quo supra (1484) in vigilia margrete (July 12) admissi sunt ad baccalariatus gradum subnotati et ordine infra scripto *(sic)* per temptatores locati
(1.) Petrus Textori de Winheim

(2.) ......etc.

(16.) Jeorius de Helmstat
Altogether 17 candidates, ranked according to their performance. The *promotor* of Helmstetter was "magister Syrus" (Syrus Lubler de Geppingen, at Heidelberg since 1471, twice dean, once vice chancellor, graduated as theologian). The dean of the faculty was Bartholomeus Egan de Calw. The class belonged to the *via moderna*. UAH I, 3, No. 49, fol. 114r. (Akten der Artistenfakultät, vol. 2, 1445-1501).

[4] "In vigilia purificationis Marie (February 1) eiusdem anni (1487)... Preterea iniunctum erat Georio de Helmstadt, qui solum bis magistris ordinarie respondit, quod in proxima disputatione ante suum temptamen tertiam responsionem compleat." UAH I, 3, No. 49, fol. 123r. "Jeorius Helmstadt" received his degree with Jodocus Brechtel as dean of the faculty of Arts. Toepke, *Matrikel*, II, p. 416. "Anno quo supra (1487) xx die mensis Martii magister Jeorius Helmstadt prestitit iuramentum pro introitu liberaie *(sic)* inferioris" UAH I, No. 49, fol. 123r. If Georgius Helmstetter had not left Heidelberg after the expiration of his obligation to teach two years, there is reason to suppose that he left sometime soon thereafter. In June, 1490, a plague broke out in Heidelberg, and all teachers and faculty members received permission to leave the city. (Toepke, I, p. 397). On October 9, 1492, the man who was soon to become court astrologer of Elector Phillip, Magister Johannes Virdung von Haßfurt, registered at the University of Heidelberg. (Toepke, I, p. 403). From a letter Johannes Trithemius wrote about Faustus to this person it is known that Virdung was not acquainted with Faustus and that he was eager to meet him. (Cf. Palmer and More, pp. 83-6). Therefore, Helmstetter was probably no longer in the city when Virdung made it the place of his permanent residence.

[5] Kaufmann, *Geschichte*, II, p. 304.
[6] Wilhelm Wattenbach, "Hartmann Schedel als Humanist," *Forschungen zur deutschen Geschichte*, 11 (1871), 351-74.
[7] Frank Baron, *Stephan Hoest: Reden und Briefe. Quellen zur Geschichte der Scholastik und des Humanismus im 15. Jahrhundert* (München: Fink, 1971), p. 74. Jos. Wils, *Matricule de L'Université de Louvain* (Brussel, 1946), II, p. 181.
[8] Hans Henning assumes that Faustus was born in approximately 1480. He does not explain the reasons for making this assumption. In fact, Faustus could have been born much earlier.
[9] Baron, *Stephan Hoest*, pp. 35-58.
[10] Karl Morneweg, *Johannes von Dalberg. Ein deutscher Humanist und Bischof* (Heidelberg: Winter, 1887), p. 30 ff.
[11] Gerhard Ritter, *Die Heidelberger Universität. Ein Stück deutscher Geschichte* (Heidelberg, 1936), pp. 468-9.
[12] "...besonders war es Agricola, der Celtis ermunterte, das Griechische und Hebräische zu erlernen, wozu er ihm ohne Zweifel selbst behilflich war, indem der Wormser Bischof (Dalberg) ihn für das Studium der platonischen Philosophie gewann..." Joseph Aschbach, "Die frühen Wanderjahre des Conrad Celtes und die Anfänge der von ihm errichteten gelehrten Sodalitäten," *Sitzungsberichte der Akademie der Wissenschaften in Wien. Philos.-historische Klasse* 60 (1968), 84. Ritter, p. 479. Morneweg, pp. 154-5, and Ludwig Geiger, *Johannes Reuchlins Briefwechsel* (Tübingen, 1875), pp. 40-1. Trithemius studied in Heidelberg in the early 1480s. He recalled later that his studies in Hebrew had begun there. When he became abbot of Sponheim he had his Heidelberg tutor of Hebrew, whom he had had to leave behind when he entered the monastery in 1482, come to Sponheim. Klaus Arnold, *Johannes Trithemius (1462-1516)*, in: *Quellen und Forschungen zur Geschichte des Bistums und Hochstifts Würzburg* (Würzburg: Schöningh, 1971), pp. 9-10 and 78-81. A manuscript from Trithemius' library indicates that he used knowledge of Hebrew to delve into the occult, and his writings show, more so than those of his humanistic associates at Heidelberg, a very intense preoccupation with this field. Cf. Paul Leh-

mann, "Merkwürdigkeiten des Abtes Johannes Trithemius," *Sitzungsberichte der Bayerischen Akademie in München. Philos.-historische Klasse* (1961), 33.
13 August Thorbecke, *Die älteste Zeit der Universität Heidelberg. 1386-1449* (Heidelberg, 1886), p. 84; Ritter, *Die Heidelberger Universität*, p. 164; Eduard Winkelmann, *Urkundenbuch der Universität Heidelberg* (Heidelberg, 1886), I, pp. 34 and 42.
14 The dangerous arts are *nigromantia* and *ars notoria* (i.e., evoking effects by means of talismans and celestially activated statues). Thorbecke, pp. 71 and 84; Ritter, p. 165.
15 Lynn Thorndike, "A Personal Memorandum by Conrad Buitzius. 1422-1427," *Speculum* 4 (1929), 88-9.
16 Hugo Holstein, "Heidelbergensia," *Zeitschrift für vergleichende Literaturgeschichte* 5 (1892), 391.
17 Karl Bartsch, *Die altdeutschen Handschriften der Universitätsbibliothek Heidelberg* (Heidelberg: Koester, 1881), see especially nos. 7, 9, 265, 276, 285, 313, 316, 330, 331 in vol. 1 and nos. 12 and 298 in vol. 2. One of the early representatives of the humanistic movement in Heidelberg, Matthias von Kemnat († 1476), court chaplain of the Elector, was an active astrologer, and a number of his astrological manuscripts have survived. In the Bayerische Staatsbibliothek, Munich, Clm. 1817 and in the Bibliotheca Vaticana Cod. Pal. lat. 1370. Conrad Celtis also studied what he referred to as "mathematics," and in Vienna he became the head of the so-called *collegium poetarum et mathematicarum*, an association that brought together humanism, astronomy, and astrology. Further evidence of interest in astrology is found in the correspondence of Celtis, Dalberg, and Reuchlin.

Notes – III. Faustus and his Contemporaries – Johannes Trithemius

1 Arnold, pp. 6-7 and 11.
2 "Hec ideo dixerim, ut si forte aliquando ad te rumor pervenerit me scire impossibilia non me magum ilico existimes sed philosophum." In the introduction to Johannes Trithemius, *Libri Polygraphiae VI* (Strasbourg: Lazarus Zetzner, 1600). The text edited by Volk shows *prophetam* instead of *philosophum*. Perhaps Volk made a mistake in deciphering an abbreviation. Cf. P. Volk, "Abt Johannes Trithemius," *Rheinische Vierteljahrsblätter* 27 (1962), 44.
3 "Eadem nocte astitit michi quidam, qui dixit, non sunt vana, Trithemi, que cogitasti quamquam tibi sint impossibilia, que nec tu nec alius tecum poteris inuenire, dixitque ad eum: Si possibilia, dic obsecro, quomodo fiant. Et aperiens os suum de singulis me per ordinem docuit ostendens, quomodo fieri, que cogitaveram multis diebus frustra facile possent." Volk, p. 44.
4 Arnold, pp. 180-4 and Isidor Silbernagl, *Johannes Trithemius* (Regensburg, 1885), pp. 93-101.
5 The third book of the *Steganographia*, "which is unfinished, does not, like the other two, contain any examples of enciphered messages; one is told to say the message over the picture of a planetary angel at a moment determined by complicated astrological calculations." D. P. Walker, *Spiritual and Demonic Magic from Ficino to Companella* (London: Warburg Inst., 1958), p. 87. Cf. Arnold, pp. 187-95.
6 Appended to Johannes Trithemius, *De Septem secundeis* (Köln: J. Bickmann, 1568), pp. 81-116.
7 "Ad unitatem reducendus omnino est ternarius, si mens harum rerum velit intellectum consequi perfectum. Unarius enim non est numerus, et ex quo ipse numerus omnis consurgit. Rejcitatur binarius, et ternarius ad unitatem convertibilis erit. Verum o Germane, ut Hermes inquit, sine mendacio certum, et unitatis cognitione verissimum." Johannes Trithemius, *Epistolarum familiarum libri duo* (Hagenau: P. Brubach, 1536), pp. 89-90. For the possible sources of this

thought see Ernst Bindel, *Pythagoras. Leben und Lehre in Wirklichkeit und Legende* (Stuttgart: Rastatt, 1962), p. 122 and Joseph Blue, *The Christian Interpretation of Cabala in the Renaissance* (New York: Columbia Univ. Press, 1944), p. 54. Arnold doesn't treat this aspect of Trithemius' thought adequately. Cf. Silbernagl, pp. 129-30. "Germanus de Ganay was *conseiller clerc* to the Parlement in 1485, canon of Notre Dame in 1486, dean of Beauvais before 1497, bishop designate of Cahors in 1509, of Orléans in 1512, and he died in 1520." Thorndike, IV, p. 514.

8 "Zuerst soll sich im Kern des Weltganzen das Feuer der Mitte gebildet haben, die Pythagoreer nennen es das Eins oder die Monas, weil es der erste Weltkörper ist, die Göttermutter . . . weil es der Mittelpunkt ist, in dem die welterhaltende Kraft ihren Sitz hat." Bindel, p. 122. Cf. pp. 104 and 121. To Johannes von Westenburg Trithemius wrote: "Ternarius enim numerus ad unitatem reductus per aspectum omnia in se continet et quae vult potest." *De septem secundeis*, p. 95. To Joachim von Brandenburg he explained: "Imprimis necessarium est, ut a natura sit ad istam artem non solum inclinatus sed et dispositus aut saltem praeceptoris magisterio disponibilis per rectificationem a ternario in unitatem per binarium divisum." Ibid, p. 110. See also letter to Libanus Gallus, footnote no. 16 below.

9 Frances A. Yates, *Giordano Bruno and the Hermetic Tradition* (Chicago: Univ. of Chicago Press, 1964), pp. 13-80.

10 Yvo Fischer, "Der Nachlaß des Abtes Johannes Trithemius von St. Jakob in Würzburg," *Archiv des Historischen Vereins für Unterfranken und Aschaffenburg*, 67 (1928), 60-5.

11 Yates, p. 146. Pico, *De dignitate hominis* (Bad Homburg: Gehlen, 1968), pp. 68-70.

12 Ibid., p. 78. Cf. footnote No. 47.

13 Arnold, p. 50.

14 Trithemius included an excerpt of a letter of Libanus ("Ex epistola Libanii Galli platonici viri doctissimi") in *De vera conversione mentis ad Deum* (Mainz: ca. 1500), f. CIII. Trithemius admits his debt to Libanius, giving biographical information, in *Nepiachus*, published in J. G. Eckhard (ed.) *Corpus historicum Medii Aevi* (Leipzig, 1723), col. 830. Cf. F. Secret, "Qui etait Libanius Gallus, le maître de Jean Tritheme?" *Estudios Lulianos* 6 (1962), 127-37. Another, less well-known teacher of Libanius was Pelagius or Ferdinando de Cordoba. Arnold, pp. 80-1.

15 Secret, pp. 132-3- Also in *Epist. famil.*, pp. 97-99.

16 ". . . ternarium pro viribus ad unitatem reducens . . ." Secret, p. 136. *Epist. famil.*, p. 341.

17 "Alchimici quidem promittunt in corporibus compositis, sed errant, fallunter, & decipiunt omnes, à quibus libenter fuerint auditi. Volunt imitari naturam, & facere partes quod solius est uniuersalis, cum radicem virtutis naturae non intelligant . . . Nostra philosophia coelestis est non terrena, ut summum illud principium quod Deum nuncupamus . . . aspiciamus . . . Abeant homines temerarii, homines uani, & mendaces astrologi, deceptores mentium, & friuola garientes. Nihil enim ad mentem immortalem, nihil ad scientiam naturalem, nihil facit ad sapientiam supercelestem stellarum dispositio, sed corpus in corpus duntaxat suum habet imperium. Mens est libera, nec stellis subiicitur, nec earum influentias conciptit, nec motum sequitur, sed supercelesti principio, à quo & facta est & foecundatur, tantum communicat." Ibid., pp. 90-3.

18 "Studium generat cognitionem, cognitio autem parit amorem, amor similitudinem, similitudo communionem, communio uirtutem, uirtus dignitatem, dignitas potentiam, & potentia facit miraculum. Hoc iter unicum ad finem magicarum . . . Ibid., p. 92.

19 Frank Borchardt, "Trithemius and the Mask of Janus," in *Traditions and Transitions. Studies in Honor of Harold Jantz*, ed. by L. E. Kurth et al. (München: Delp, 1972), p. 46.

20 D. P. Walker treats the complicated problems arising from the proximity of these two areas of interest: "The historical importance of these connections between magic and religion is, I think, that they led people to ask questions about religious practices and experiences which would not otherwise have occurred to them; and, by approaching religious problems through magic, which

was at least partially identical with, or exactly analogous to religion, but which could be treated without reverence or devotion, they were able sometimes to suggest answers which, whether true or not, were new and fruitful." Walker, p. 84.

[21] Arnold, pp. 201-8 and Silbernagl, pp. 101-12.

[22] "...Nihil feci stupendum, et tamen vulgi opinionem patior, dum magum me plerique arbitrantur, assuerantes me suscitasse mortuos, evocasse ab inferis daemones, praedixisse futura, furesque reduxisse carminibus et ligasse latrones." *Epist. famil.*, p. 303. At the same time Trithemius wrote elsewhere: "Multos enim et magnus de me rumor apud plures exivit, nescio quibus occasionibus, quod sciam, fecerimque miranda per nescio quas artes, aut quorum spirituum, suscitaverim mortuos, recuperaverim furta, praedixerim futura, ostenderimque mirabilia, quae omnia conficta sunt et falsa..." *Nepiachus*, col. 829.

[23] Gustav Bauch, "Deutsche Scholaren in Krakau in der Zeit der Renaissance. 1460 bis 1520," *Jahresbericht der Schlesischen Gesellschaft für väterländische Kultur* (1901), 31.

[24] Karl Hartfelder, "Der Aberglaube Philipp Melanchthons," *Historisches Taschenbuch*, 6 (1889), 245.

[25] "Ad magistrum ioannem virdungi de hasfurdia mathematicum serenissimi principis philippi palatini comitis. Ioannes tritemius abbas monasterii sancti iacobi in suburbano civitatis herbipolensis: ioanni virdungo de hasfurt mathematico expertissimo salutem. Exhibuit mihi literas tuas heinricus gronigerus reuerendissimi presulis nostri a secretis: quibus plane cognoui causam meam petitoriam apud serenissimum principem philippum comitem palatinum per te fuisse promotum. Quare tibi gratias habeo quam maximas: referamque pro viribus quotiens mihi dabitur occasio. De libris uero principis faciam iuxta consilium tuum: quamuis timeam ne mora inducat periculum: quoniam homines sunt uigilancia ut plurimum carentes qui paruam rebus eciam ardius adhibeant curam. Librum uero tuum quem mihi comodasti manibus commisi scriptoris: qui mox ut fuerit rescriptus ad te sine mora reuertetur. Libros autem berengarii meos quos apud te budoris rescribendos: cum perfeceris ad me ut redeant iubeto. Homo ille de quo mihi scripsisti georgius sabellicus qui se principem necromanticorum ausus est nominare, gyrouagus battologus et circumcelio est: dignus qui verberibus castigetur: ne temere deinceps tam nephanda et ecclesie sancte contraria publice audeat profiteri. Quid enim sunt aliud tituli quos sibi assumit: nisi stultissime ac uesane mentis indicia: quibus se fatuum non philosophum ostendit. Sic enim titulum sibi conuenientem formavit. Magister georgius sabellicus faustus iunior, fons necromanticorum, astrologus, magus secundus chyromanticus agromanticus pyromanticus in hydra arte secundus. Vide stultum hominis temeritatem quanta feratur insania ut se fontem necromancie profiteri presumat: qui vere omnium bonarum literarum ignarus fatuum se pocius appellare debuisset quam magistrum. Sed me non latet eius nequicia. Cum anno priore de marchia brandenburgensi redirem hunc ipsum hominem apud geilenhausen oppidum inueni: de quo mihi plura dicebantur in hospicio frivola non sine magna eius temeritate ab eo promissa. Qui mox ut me adesse audiuit fugit hospicio: et a nullo poterat persuaderi quod se meis presentaret aspectibus. Titulum stulticie sue qualem dedit ad te quem memorauimus per quendam civem ad me quoque destinauit. Referebant mihi quidam in oppido sacerdotes quod in multorum presencia dixit tantam se omnis sapiencie consecutum scienciam atque memoriam ut si volumina platonis et aristotelis omnia cum tota eorum philosophia in toto perisset ab hominum memoria: ipse suo ingenio velut ezras alter hebreus restituere universa cum prestanciore valeret elegancia. Postea me neometi existente herbipolim venit eademque vanitate actus in plurimorum fertur dixisse presencia: quod christi saluatoris miracula non sint miranda: se quoque omnia facere posse que christus fecit, quotiens et quandocumque velit. In ultima quoque huius anni quadragesima venit stauronesum et simili stulticia gloriosus de se pollicebatur ingencia, dicens se in alchimia omnium qui ferint vmquam esse perfectissimum et scire atque posse quicquid homines optauerint. Vacabat interea munus docendi scolasticum in oppido memorato ad quod francisci de sickingen baliui

principis tui hominis mysticarum rerum percupidi promocione fuit assumptus: qui mox nefandissimo fornicacionis genere cum pueris videlicet voluptari cepit: quo statim deducto in lucem: fuga penam declinauit paratam. Hec sunt que mihi certissimo constant testimoni de homine illo que tantouent uenturum esse desiderio prestolaris. Cum uencrit ad te: non philosophum sed hominem fatuum et nimia temeritate agitatum invenies. Vale mei memor cum oportunitate principali. Ex herbipoli. xx. die mensis augusti. Anno christianorum. M.D. vii." Cod. Pal. lat. 730, fol. 174-175. Printed in *Epist. famil.*, pp. 312-314. I have not made changes in the Latin text. For the translation cf. Palmer and More, pp. 83-6.

26 For the chronology of these events see Silbernagl, pp. 109-10. From Arnold's presentation one might have the impression that Trithemius was in Gotha before he went to Leipzig. Arnold, p. 207.
27 Henning, p. 116. Erich Schmidt, "Zur Vorgeschichte des Goethe'schen Faust," *Goethe-Jahrbuch* 3 (1882), 97.
28 Trithemius enumerated the demonic arts in a defense of natural magic: "... necromantia, piromantia, acromantia, idromantia, geomantia, chiromantia, orincomantia, sortilegium, eromantia, maleficius..." *Nepiachus*, col. 830.
29 Trechard's reference to acromancy is quoted in Burton Feldmann and Robert D. Richardson, *The Rise of Modern Mythology* (Bloomington: Indiana University Press, 1972), p. 37. Professor Hans Eggers, who was kind enough to try to help me with this puzzle, suggested the possibility that *agromanticus* was formed on the basis of the Greek word ἄκρος.
30 "Magorum primus Zoroastes rex Bactrianorum..." Isidor, *Etymol.* VIII, ix. "Nam (Zoroastes) magicarum artium fuisse perhibetur inventor." Augustine, *De civitate Dei*, XXI, xiv. The same view is expressed by Pico. Yates, p. 15.
31 "Nam ipse Numa... hydromantian facere compulsus est, ut in aqua videret imagines deorum vel potius ludificationes daemonum..." Augustine, *De civitate Dei*, VII, xxxv.
32 See footnote No. 15 in chapter I.
33 Wilfred P. Mustard, ed., *The Eclogues of Faustus Andrelinus and Ioannes Arnolletus* (Baltimore: Johns Hopkins Univ. Press, 1918), pp. 11-19.
34 Frater Johannes Cordiger in Ulm in the introduction of Faustus' *Livia*, published in 1490. Mustard, p. 14.
35 This work was published in Paris by Guy Marchant.
36 Gustav Schwetschke, "Wer war Faustus senior?" *Deutsches Museum* (1855), 548-551. Hermann Grimm, "Die Entstehung des Volksbuches vom Dr. Faust," *Preußische Jahrbücher* 47 (1881), 455.
37 Paul Melcher, "Die Bedeutung des Konrad Celtis für die Namenforschung," *Namenforschung, Fests. f. A. Bach*, R. Schützeicherl (ed.), (Heidelberg, Winter 1965), pp. 160-7.
38 Johannes Trithemius, *Liber octo questionum ad Maximilianum Caesarem* (Oppenheim: J. Hasselberg, 1515), fol. Fi^v-Fii^v.
39 Trithemius thus assumed that Faustus' title *magister* clearly implied master of philosophy.
40 Dieter Harmening argues that Faustus associated himself with Ezra and that this implies that Faustus himself practiced cabala. Dieter Harmening, "Faust und die Renaissance-Magie. Zum ältesten Fauszeugnis," *Archiv für Kulturgeschichte* 55 (1973), pp. 65-6.
41 Eusebius, *The Ecclesiastical History*, trs. by K. Lake (London: Heinemann, 1926), I, p. 461.
42 "Esdras propheta libros Mosi combustos a Caldeis, qui et Babylonii fuerunt dicti, memoria usus pro archetypo reparavit." *De septem secundeis*, p. 29.
43 H. Ulmann, *Franz von Sickingen* (Leipzig: Hirzel, 1872), pp. 8-10. Ernst Münch, *Franz von Sickingens Thaten, Pläne, Freunde und Ausgang* (Aachen: Mayer, 1829), III, p. 223-4.
44 Sickingen wrote of Reuchlin: "... er sich so vil an jme gewesen beflissen hat, mich in meiner jugent sittlicher tugent zo unterweisen." Edward Böcking, *Hutteni opera* (Leipzig: Teubner,

1864), suppl. I, p. 438. Hutten said, however, that Sickingen was "sine literis." Ulmann, p. 10.
45 "Huis vestigia secutus usque ab adolescentia prima filius rei magicae deditus, ne ulla re patris esset dissimilis, inter alia maleficia, quae ipse Reipublicae iniussit, haec sane literis ac omnium sermonibus celebrata." Because of the late date of this report, it is conceivable that its ultimate source was Trithemius. P. Christopher Brower and Jacob Masen, *Antiquitatum et annalium Trevirensium libri XXV* (Liège, 1670), p. 337.
46 "Wiewol obgenannter Juncker Franz von Sickingen ohn Haßfurts Prognostication und Rath, kein fürtrefflich fürnehmen oder Handlung unterstanden, als ich berichtet, sich gemeiniglich an Haßfurdts Rath gehalten..." Chr. Goth. Neudecker and Ludwig Preller, *Georg Spalatins historischer Nachlaß und Briefe* (Jena: F. Mauke, 1851), p. 188. Cf. Münch, II, pp. 319-21 and Ulmann, pp. 274-5. Adam Wernher was Spalatin's brother-in-law. He made a copy of the original horoscope, found among the papers of Sickingen after the latter's death.
47 Harmening, pp. 66-9.

Notes – III. Faustus and his Contemporaries – Mutianus

1 Karl Gillert, ed., *Der Briefwechsel des Conrad Mutianus*, Geschichtsquellen der Provinz Sachsen, 18 (Halle: O. Handel, 1890), pp. VIII-XXXIV. Carl Krause, ed., *Der Briefwechsel des Mutianus Rufus* (Kassel: A. Freyschmidt, 1885), pp. I-VIII.
2 Arnold, pp. 98-9.
3 Gillert, pp. 29-30.
4 Ibid., pp. 2-3.
5 Ibid., pp. 382-3.
6 Krause, pp. XXXIV and 102.
7 Gillert, pp. 258-60.
8 Ibid., pp. 53-5 and p. 304.
9 Ibid., pp. 258-60. "... quidquid in mundo scibile est, scire semper cupiebam." J. Trithemius, *Nepiachus*, col. 1829.
10 Gillert, pp. 304-5.
11 "Delectatur etiam magorum honestioribus mysteriis, que tibi penitus perspecta sunt et cognita." Ibid., pp. 382-3. Arnold, p. 99.
12 Ibid., 382.
13 "Venit octauo abhinc die quidam chiromanticus Erphurdiam nomine georgius faustus helmitheus hedelbergensis merus ostentator et fatuus. Eius et omnium diuinaculorum vana est professio et talis physiognomia leuior typula. Rudes admirantur. In eum theologi insurgant. Non conficiant philosophum Capnionem. Ego audiui garrientem in hospitio. Non castigaui iactantiam. Quid aliena insania ad me?" Cod. lat. oct. 8, fol. 96^v-97^r. For the English text see Palmer and More pp. 87-8.

Notes – III. Faustus and his contemporaries – Bishop of Bamberg

1 He registered in the summer semester of 1486. "Dominus Georgius baro in Limpurg sacri imperii pincerna hereditarius, Argentinensis, Bambergensis et Herbipolensis ecclesiarum canonicus dedit duos florenos." Götz Freiherr von Pölnitz, *Die Matrikel der Ludwig Maximilians-Uni-

versität (München: J. Lindau, 1937), p. 163. According to Guttenberg, Georg Schenck von Limpurg was studying in Ingolstadt also in 1493. Erich Frhr. von Guttenberg, *Das Bistum Bamberg* in *Germania sacra* (Berlin, de Gruyter, 1933), p. 280.

2 "Georius, baro baronie Lympurg sacri Romani imperii heres, pincerna, semperfry, ecclesiarum Argentinensis, Bambergensis et Herbipolensis canonicus." Hans Georg Wackernagel, *Die Matrikel der Universität Basel* (Basel: Werner und Bischoff, 1951), I, p. 213.

3 Franz Friedrich Leitschuh, *Georg III., Schenk von Limpurg, der Bischof von Bamberg in Goethes Götz von Berlichingen* (Bamberg: F. Züberlein, 1888). Cf. Chr. Beck, "Der Bamberger Frühhumanist Leonhard von Egloffstein," *Beiträge zur Bayerischen Kirchengeschichte* 29 (1923), p. 13 ff.

4 *Allgemeine Deutsche Biographie*, vol. 33, pp. 305-6.

5 Gustav C. Knod, *Deutsche Studenten in Bologna* (Berlin: Decker, 1899), pp. 141-2. Johannes Kist, *Die Matrikel des Bistums Bamberg. 1400-1556* (Würzburg: Schöningh, 1965), nos. 1874 and 1878.

6 Leitschuh, pp. 14-6.

7 Kist, no. 832.

8 Leitschuh, pp. 18-20.

9 Karl Schottenloher, "Johann Schöner und seine Hausdruckerei," *Zentralbibliothek für Bibliothekswesen* 24 (1907), p. 145.

10 Emil Reicke, "Der Bamberger Kanonikus Lorenz Beheim, Pirckheimers Freund," *Forschungen zur Geschichte Bayerns* 14 (1906), pp. 44-5.

11 Ibid., p. 8.

12 Kist, no. 4441. Dr. Mistele, Oberarchivrat of the Staatsarchiv Bamberg, was kind enough to supply me with the following information: "Der Kammermeister Hans Müller amtierte von 1517 bis 1524, was sich etwa mit einem Teil der Zeit, in der Johann Molitoris (Müller) nachgewiesen ist, deckt. In der Regel war der Kammermeister ein weltlicher Beamter, während der bei Kist genannte Molitoris immerhin Geistlicher und promovierter Jurist gewesen ist, so daß einiges gegen die Identität der beiden Personen spricht."

13 "Item X guld(en) geben vnd geschenckt doctor faustus ph(ilosoph)o zuuererung hat m(einem) g(nedigen) Herrn ein natiuitet oder Iudicium gemacht. Zalt am Sontag nach scolastice. Iussit R(everendissi)mus." Stadtarchiv Bamberg, "Hofkammerrechnungen des Kreisarchivs Bamberg, pro diversis," (H 231, 1741). For the English text see Palmer and More, pp. 88-9.

14 Leitschuh, pp. 77 and 90.

15 For drawing my attention to the possible connection between the consultation with Faustus and the Bishop's concern about death I am indebted to Sonja Thom. Cf. Leitschuh, p. 88.

16 Leitschuh, p. 65.

Notes – III. Faustus and his Contemporaries – Kilian Leib

1 Cf. the preface to *Annales maiores* in Johann Christ. Frhr. von Aretin, *Beiträge zur Geschichte und Literatur* (München: Scherer, 1806), p. 537 and Andreas Straus, *Viri scriptis, eruditione ac pietate insignes, quos Eichstadium vel genuit vel aluit* (Eichstätt, 1799), p. 262.

2 Emil Reicke et al. (ed.), *Willibald Pirckheimers Briefwechsel* (München: C. H. Beck, 1940), I, pp. 175 ff.

3 Josef Deutsch, *Kilian Leib, Prior von Rebdorf. Ein Lebensbild aus dem Zeitalter der deutschen Reformation* (Münster: 1910), p. 26.

4 Kilian Leyb, *Gründtliche Anzaygung und Bericht auß was Ursachen (deren fürnemlich siben*

seind) so mancherlay / und vilfaltige Ketzereyen / zwispaltung und jrrthumb in Christlicher Religion / und der hailigen Catholischen Kirchen / von Anfang biß auff dise Zeit erwachsen seind / und jren grund genommen haben (Ingolstadt: S. Wessenhorn, 1557). Leib gives the time of composition in chapter VI as January, 1528. Cf. fol. CXXVII-CXXVII^v.

5 Leib mistakenly thought that he was using Regiomontanus as his source. Schottenloher feels that this was an important factor in causing Leib to take the opinion seriously. Karl Schottenloher, "Der Rebdorder Prior Kilian Leib und sein Wettertagebuch von 1513 bis 1531," in *Riezler-Festschrift* ed. by Karl Alexander von Müller, *Beiträge zur bayerischen Geschichte* (Gotha, 1913), p. 94.

6 "Ich habe nun bey fünfftzehn jarn wie es alle tag gewittert oder wann es geregnet hat / germerckt und aufgezaichnet / und darauß erfarn unnd gefunden / das die Astronomey / auch die bawrn mit jren Prophetisiern des Wetters halben nit besteen / und offt ernider ligen." K. Leib, *Gründtliche Anzaygung*, fol. XCVIII^v-XCIX.

7 Ibid., fol. XCVIII^v-XCIX.
8 Ibid., fol. CXIII.
9 Ibid., fol. CIV^v-CV.
10 Ibid., fol. CXXXIII. Cf. Deutsch, p. 75.
11 *Gründtliche Anzaygung*, fol. CXLI^v-CXLII.
12 "Georgius faustus helmstet(ensis) quinta Junii dicebat, qunado sol et Jupiter sunt in eodem unius signi gradu, tunc nascuntur prophete (utpote sui similes). Asserebat se commendatorem seu praecptorem domunculae Johannitarum in confiniis carintiae, quod appeletur hallestein." Bayerische Staatsbibliothek München, 4° L. impr. c. n. mss. 73, fol. 257^r. For the English text see Palmer and More, p. 89.
13 Aby Warburg, "Heidnisch-antike Weissagung in Wort und Bild zu Luthers Zeiten," in *Gesammelte Schriften* (Leipzig, 1932), II, pp. 487-558.
14 *Commendator sive praeceptor* was the accurate form for a very specific position of authority over a so-called commandery. "The rulers of these small houses were referred to most commonly as commanders or preceptors, but they were also called priors, masters or procurators ... In these commanderies there lived a variable number of brethren in convent; there was a church and the whole was governed by a commander." Jonathan Riley-Smith, *The Knights of St. John in Jerusalem and Cyprus* (London: MacMillan, 1967), p. 341. "The commanders were for the most part Knights, but a due proportion of commanderies was reserved for the chaplains and serving brothers of arms." E. J. King, *The Knights of St. John in the British Empire* (London: St. John's Gate, 1934), p. 82. My knowledge about the holdings of the Prague archives is based on a general catalogue of its Neo-Latin manuscripts. Václav Cerný, "Les manuscrites en langues néolatines de la Bibliothèque du Grand Prieuré de l'Ordre des Chevalier de Malte à Prague," *Sborník Národního muzea v Praze. (Acta Musei Nationalis Pragae)*, Series 3, 8 (1963), pp. 109-69. The State Archives in Prague have given me the following reply to my inquiries about their holdings: "Dokumente, die sich auf Kommende Haillenstein *(sic)* im Archiv des böhmischen Großpriorats des Malteserordens beziehen, beginnen erst im Jahre 1564; wir können also keine Angaben über Georgius Faustus vorlegen." The Order of St. John has its central archives on the Island of Malta. Fr. Jos. Mizzi, director, was kind enough to supply me with the following information: "I have looked at the LIBRI BULLARUM for the years 1526-34 in which the official chancery copy of the Bull appointing Dr. Faustus to the Preceptory or Commandery of Heilenstein, if it existed, ought to be found. I regret to inform you that I did not come across any notice relating to Dr. Faustus."
15 "Anheut Mitwoch nach viti 1528. Dem Wahrsager sol befohlen werden, daß er zu der Stadt auszieh und seinen Pfennig anderswo verzehre." (Ratsprotokoll über die obrigkeitlichen Beschlüsse); "Am Mitwoch nach viti 1528 ist einem der sich genannt doctor Jörg Faustus von Haidlberg

gesagt, daß er seinen Pfennig anderswo verzehre, und hat angelobt, solche Erforderung für die Obrigkeit nicht zu ahnden noch zu äffern." (Ratsprotokoll, Verwiesenen). Both items to be found in the Stadtarchiv Ingolstadt. For the English text see Palmer and More, p. 90.

[16] "D. Georgius Faustus zu Ingolstadt auf der hohen Schul der Studenten Philosophiam und [Ch]iromantiam lase." Wilhelm Meyer, "Nürnberger Faustgeschichten," in *Abhandlungen der Bayerischen Akademie der Wissenschaften*, class 1, 20 (1896), p. 309.

Notes – III. Faustus and his Contemporaries – Camerarius

[1] This essay on Camerarius' relationship to Faustus is a slightly revised form of an essay printed in *Joachim Camerarius (1500-1574)*, edited by Frank Baron and published in the *Humanistische Bibliothek* series of Fink Verlag. – Georg Ellinger, "Ein unbekanntes Zeugnis über den historischen Faust," *Goethe*-Jahrbuch, 10 (1889), 256-257 and "Das Zeugnis des Camerarius über Faust," *Vierteljahrschrift für Literaturgeschichte*, 2 (1889), 114-319. Friedrich Kluge elaborated on Ellinger's quotations, but because of weak documentation his assertions, even where they are correct and valuable, inspire little faith. His article was overlooked by subsequent scholars of the historical Faustus. Friedrich Kluge, "Vom geschichtlichen Dr. Faust," in: Friedrich Kluge, *Bunte Blätter. Kulturgeschichtliche Vorträge und Aufsätze* (Freiburg, 1908), pp. 1-27. The most comprehensive recent study on Faustus was that of Hans Henning, "Faust als historische Gestalt," *Jahrbuch der Goethe-Gesellschaft*, N. F. 21 (1959), 107-139. A very important work on the same subject is that of Ernst Beutler, "Georg Faust aus Helmstadt," *Goethe-Kalender* (1936), 170-210.

[2] "Doctor Fausto dem großen Sodomiten und Nigromantico in furt glait ablainen. Burgermeister iunior." Palmer and More, p. 90. The original entry is in the Nürnberg Staatsarchiv: Nüremberger Ratsverlässe, Nr. 870. f. 12.

[3] H. Knapp, *Das alte Nürnberger Kriminalrecht* (Berlin, 1896), p. 233.

[4] Palmer and More, p. 86.

[5] Melanchthon also names D. (Dominus?) Cholerus, probably Christoph Kohler. Cf. J. G. Doppelmayr, *Historische Nachricht von den Nürnbergischen Mathematicis und Künstlern* (Nürnberg: P. C. Monath 1730). Cf. Melanchthon's letter to Johannes Schöner, dated August 7, 1536, in: Philipp Melanchthon *Mathematicarum disciplinarum tum etiam astrologiae economia* (Strasbourg, 1537), fol. B7^v-C3. Also in *Corpus Reformatorum* (Henceforth CR), III, cols. 115-119. The same text was published previously as a preface to Johannes Schöner's *Tabulae astronomicae resolutae* (Nürnberg, 1536). To this list one could add still other names of well-known personalities who were versed in astrology and lived in or in the vicinity of Nuremberg: Hartmann Schedel, Martin and Lorenz Beheim, Konrad Heinfogel, and Johannes Stab. Cf. Ernst Zinner, Die *Fränkische Sternkunde im 11. bis 16.* Jahrhundert (Bamberg, 1934). Others still are named in Doppelmayr's work.

[6] Melanchthon, *Mathematicarum encomia*, fol. B8. On Schöner see the article in *Allgemeine Deutsche Biographie*, Vol. 32, pp. 295-97.

[7] Zinner, p. 79.

[8] K. Sudhoff, *Paracelsus. Ein deutsches Lebensbild aus den Tagen der Renaissance* (Leipzig, 1936), pp. 67-79.

[9] The identification of the Deputy Burgomaster was made by Dr. Matthias Thiel for the State Archives of Nuremberg. Dr. Machilek kindly supplied me with this information. Cf. Joachim Camerarius, *Epistolarum familiarum libri VI* (henceforth Ep. VI), (Frankfurt: apud haeredes Adreae Wecheli, 1583), pp. 197 and 217.

10 In August of 1529 Camerarius wrote to his friend Daniel Stibar about a doctor who was visiting Nuremberg and was a friend of Stibar. Since Stibar was known to have been a friend of Faustus it is conceivable that this letter is actually about Faustus: "Non fui apud doctorem amicum tuum. Nam cum ille mihi literas ante coenam misisset, credo quod cuperet me apud se esse ego qui non possem venire statim significavi ei, adventurum me post coenam. Retinebar autem domi cum illo inveterato malo pedis, tum cuiusdam amici praesentia. Post coenam in multam sane noctem veni in cauponam, sed ille adhuc coenabat, et occurrit mihi quidam tum metus, ut non exspectarim finam coenae. De illo metu narrabo tibi cum adveneris." Joachim Camerarius, *Epistolarum libri quinque posteriores* (henceforth Ep. V) (Frankfurt: P. Fischer, 1595), p. 119.

11 Preface of April 12, 1532 to the astrologer Andreas Perlach: "Cum te iamdiu novi e scriptis tuis Perlachi, tum mihi singularam admirationem tui excitarunt sermones amici nostri Schoneri, mathematicarum disciplinarum professoris apud nos." Joachim Camerarius, *Astrologia* (Nuremberg: J. Petrejus, 1532).

12 Ludwig Geiger, *Renaissance und Humanismus in Deutschland* (Berlin, 1882), pp. 495-98.

13 Melanchthon, *Mathematicarum encomia*, fol. 22ᵛ. Karl Hartfelder, "Der Aberglaube Philipp Melanchthons," *Historisches Taschenbuch*, 6 (1889), 240-41.

14 Robert Stupperich (edit.), *Melanchthons Werke*, VII, 1 (Gütersloh: Gerd Mohn, 1971), 240-41.

15 Melanchthon, *Mathematicarum encomia*, fol. A4.

16 Preface letter to *Astrologia:* "Nam cum inter reliquas librorum Joannis de Regiomonte reperissem unum codicem Graecum fere totum scriptum manu ipsius..." Cf. Thorndike, p. 358. Ep. VI, pp. 200-201. Schöner himself published works of Regiomontanus in 1553, 1534 and 1544.

17 Ptolemy, *Tetrabiblos*, ed. and translated by F. E. Robbins (Cambridge: Harvard University Press, 1948), pp. xi and xiii.

18 Julius Rauscher, "Der Halleysche Komet im Jahre 1531 und die Reformation," *Zeitschrift für Kirchengeschichte*, 32 (1911), 259-76. Zinner, p. 68.

19 CR II, cols. 518-57.

20 "Nobis afferet, nisi fallor, pestilentiam." Ep. V, p. 131; cf. pp. 136, 143 and (about the significance of an eclipse) 135.

21 Heinrich Wilhelm Heerwagen, *Zur Geschichte der Nürnberger Gelehrtenschule in dem Zeitraume von 1485 bis 1526* (Nuremberg, 1868), p. 7.

22 Johannes Voigt, *Briefwechsel der berühmtesten Gelehrten des Zeitalters der Reformation mit Herzog Albrecht von Preußen* (Königsberg, 1841), pp. 111-13. Cf. Walter Hubatsch, *Albrecht von Brandenburg-Ansbach* (Heidelberg, 1960), pp. 267-71.

23 Peter Gerrit Thielen, *Die Kultur am Hofe Herzog Albrechts von Preußen* (1525-1568), Göttinger Bausteine zur Geschichtswissenschaft, No. 12 (Göttingen: Musterschmidt, 1953), pp. 130 and 180.

24 CR II, cols. 505, 602, etc. *Neue Deutsche Biographie* (henceforth cited as NDB), vol. III, pp. 138-39. Aby Warburg, "Heidnisch-antike Weissagung in Wort und Bild zu Luthers Zeiten," in *Gesammelte Schriften*, II (Leipzig, 1932), p. 495. On Copernicus see Leopold Prowe, *Nicolaus Copernicus* (Berlin, 1883), II, p. 219.

25 Joachim Camerarius, *Narratio de Eobano* (Nürnberg: d. Von Bergen und U. Neuber, 1553), fol. Cᵛ. P. S. Allen, *Opus Epistolarum Des. Erasmi Roterdami* (Oxford, 1922-28), vol. 4, p. 615 and vol. 7, p. 528.

26 Stibar became judge *(Landrichter)* for Franconia in 1538. He died in 1555. Eva Mayer, "Daniel Stiebar von Buttenheim und Joachim Camerarius," *Würzburger Diözesangeschichtsblätter*, 14 (1952), 485-99. Comprehensive biographical and bibliographical information on Stibar is to be found in Stupperich, pp. 232-33. Cf. August Amrhein, "Reihenfolge der Mitglieder des adligen Domstiftes zu Würzburg," *Archiv des historischen Vereins für Unterfranken und Aschaffenburg*, 33 (1890), 335. Camerarius wrote a biographical sketch of Stibar in the preface to his *Hippocomi-*

cus (Leipzig: V. Papst, 1556).
27 Allen, vol. 4, p. 615. Hutten had studied at the universities of Leipzig (registered in the SS 1518), Ingolstadt (registered in the WS 1520) and Padua. At the age of 13 he held a minor office. At the same time he had very close ties to the Church in Eichstätt. He was canon of both Würzburg and Eichstätt when he registered at the University of Freiburg in 1929. Karl Ried, *Moritz von Hutten. Fürstbischof von Eichstätt (1539) und die Glaubensspaltung* (Münster, 1925). Andreas Straus, *Viri scriptis, eruditione ac pietate insignes, quos Eichstadium vel genuit vel aluit* (Eichstätt, 1799), pp. 305-10. Cf. Hermann Meyer (ed.), *Die Matrikel der Universität Freiburg* (Freiburg, 1910), I, p. 277. Amrhein, pp. 163-64.
28 Eduard Böcking, *Ulrichs von Hutten Schriften* (1859-1861), repr. Aalen, 1963), II, pp. 355-63 and 446. David Friedrich Strauß, *Ulrich von Hutten* (Leipzig, 1914), pp. 462-63.
29 Mayer, pp. 487-87.
30 The interest of Moritz von Hutten in these matters is reflected in a book dedicated to him by Jacob Kubel. Besides being very favorable and flattering to Charles V it contains a poem about prophecy. Jacob Kubel, *Elegia in fine continens vaticinium* (s.l., 1547). In locating this rare book I had the kind help of Dr. Schneiders of the Bayerische Staatsbibliothek.
31 Camerarius to Stibar on March 5, 1536: "Fuit apud nos Mauricius Huttenus, attulitque iucundissimum nuncium adventus tui. Utinam modo nihil interveniat, quo ille impediatur. Collacuti (ut solemus) de variis sumus, et praebebatur locuples occasio sermonum de literis Philippi fratris illius proficientis cum Velseriana classe Indiam. Ab eo accepi hunc fasciculum literarum curandum tibi." Ep. V, pp. 144-45.
32 Camerarius wrote to Stibar: "Iam transiens hac et praeteriens meas aedes, salutavit me de equo Philippus Huttenus cum fratre, narravitque mihi Mauricium convalescere, quo sum valde delectatus." Ep. V, p. 119.
33 According to a report of Barthalomeus Welser to the Emperor: "... Philipp von Hutten (welcher von Jugend auf an Euer Kayl. Mt. Hof, von dem wohlgebohrnen Herrn Heinrichen Grafen von Naussau etc. unserm lieben Freund und gnädigen Herrn erzogen, und folgendes wie er erwachsen Euer Kayl. Mt. Diener worden)..." "Zeitung aus India," *Historisch-Literarisches Magazin*, 1 (1785), p. 112. For letters of Heinrich von Nassau with references to Hutten see Johannes Wilhelm von Arnoldi, "Briefe aus dem sechzehnten Jahrhundert," in J. W. von Arnoldi, *Historische Denkwürdigkeiten* (Leipzig, 1817), pp. 216-17.
34 Joachim Camerarius, *Erratum* (Nuremberg: Johannes Petrejus, 1535). Heerwagen's reference to March of 1536 as the time of the first publication is not correct. He was thinking of the later Basel edition. Heerwagen, p. 21.
35 The poem is entitled "Joachimi Camerarii Aeolia, ad clarissimum virum Mauricium Huttenum."

    Sic liquido coepta auspicio quemcunque habitura
    Sunt finem, finis non erit malus.

Joachim Camerarius, *Erratum* (Basel: B. Lasius and T. Platter, 1536), fol. 17^v. Subsequent excerpts from the poem are also from this edition. On the Hutten expedition see Konrad Haebler, *Die überseeischen Unternehmungen der Welser und ihrer Gesellschaftler* (Leipzig, 1903), p. 228.
36 Lines 17-18 refer to this event:

    Frater in augusta Caroli celeberrimus aula
    Gentis honor patriae, gentis honorque suae.

Erratum, fol. 18. For Hutten's own reference to the audience with Charles V see Fernando Cortes, *Von dem Newen Hispanien* (Augsburg: B. Ulhart, 1550), fol. 51.
37 Cf. lines 35-38:

Omnia sint votis terraque marique secunda,
Virtuti iuvenis nate Philippe, tuis:
Ut quondam incolumi patriaeque tuisque reverso,
Nemo sit in terra par tibi Teutonide.

Friedrich Kluge presents lines 5-6 and 35-38 together as one continuous poem. Since he does not indicate his source at all, it is impossible to say with certainty whether there is any justifiable basis for his arrangement of the lines. It is reasonable to assume that lines 5-6 do, in fact, refer to the Hutten expedition. Kluge, p. 7.

[38] Georg Ellinger, "Jakob Micyllus und Joachim Camerarius. Zwei neulateinische Dichter," *Neue Jahrbücher für das klassische Altertum, Geschichte und deutsche Literatur und für Pädagogik*, 24 (1909), 165. Georg Voigt overlooked the poem of Camerarius in his consideration of literature of the emperor's expedition against Tunis. He mentioned a poem by another famous Nuremberg resident, Hans Sachs: "Historia von dem Kaiserlichen Sieg in Königreich Tunis." Georg Voigt, "Die Geschichtschreibung über den Zug Karls V. gegen Tunis," *Abhandlung der Sächsischen Gesellschaft der Wissenschaften*, 6 (1874), 165-243.

[39] CR II, cols. 600-01; Warburg, p. 498.

[40] "Noli enim putare plus fidei habendum vllis astrologorum aut aurispicum divinationibus, quam corum qui vatum nomen proprius inuenerunt, non imbuti superstitione aliqua, sed instinctu quodam et vi caelesti praediti." Joachim Camerarius, *Commentarius captae urbis ductore Carlo Borbonio* (Basel: J. Herwagen, 1536), p. 4.

[41] Cf. footnote no. 54.

[42] "... sed ob hanc etiam caussam hoc tempore in istam editionem operam diligenter dedi, ut te inter varios rumores quasi vaticiniis quibusdam confirmarem." *Commentarius*, p. 4.

[43] Ibid., p. 4.

[44] Ibid., p. 4.

[45] Marjorie Reeves, *The Influence of Prophecy in the Later Middle Ages, A Study in Joachimism* (Oxford: Clarendon Press, 1969).

[46] Ibid., p. 508.

[47] "Haec, mi Daniele, si videbitur, communicabis cum Huteno nostro cuius fratrem Philippum natum laudi iuuenem, reuersum de Indica nauigatione, ducere aliquot ad Caesarem cohortes audimus, sumuspue illius laudatissimis conatibus precati dignam fortunam. Quam quidem iam ita ille finxit animo supra aetatem forti atque magno, ut instabilissima Dea in hoc mutari non posse videatur. Quicquid enim accidat, ego quidem volo ominorque laeta omnia." *Commentarius*, p. 5.

[48] "Hie habt ihr von allen Gubernationen ein wenig, damit ihr sehet, daß wir hie in Venezola nicht allein bissher unglücklich gewest sein, diese alle obgemelte Armata verdorben seind innerhalb 3. Monathe, vor und nach uns zu Sevilla ausgefahren, daß ich bekennen muss, daß es der Philosophus Faustus schier troffen hat, dann wir ein fast bösses Jahr antroffen haben, aber Gott hab Lob ist uns fast unter allen andern am besten gangen." "Zeitung aus India," p. 93. English text quoted from Palmer and More, pp. 95-96. According to Witkowski the prognostication of Faustus must have referred to a period of three months: "... die ungünstige Prophezeihung hat sich, wie aus Huttens Worten hervorgeht, auf die Unternehmungen des Herbstes 1534, die drei Monate, innerhalb deren er von Sevilla abfuhr, bezogen." Georg Witkowski, "Der historische Faust," *Deutsche Zeitschrift für Geschichtswissenschaft*, N. F. 1 (1896-7), 336. Against this interpretation it might be pointed out that Witkowski accounts for only three months; the text itself speaks of a year ("ein bösses Jahr").

[49] In a letter of August 18, 1550, Camerarius wrote to Stibar that he intended to write an epitaph for Philipp von Hutten. Ep. V, p. 200. This is undoubtedly the inscription on the alabaster monument erected for Philipp von Hutten in the church named Mariasondheim in Arnstein. The artist was Loy Hering. Cf. *Kunstdenkmäler von Bayern*, vol. 3, H. 6, pp. 34-35.

⁵⁰ "Zeitung aus India," p. 89. Hutten mentions a number of acquaintances to whom he would like to send greetings: "Bitt euch wollet Herrn Daniel Stieber mein Dienst sagen, desgleichen mir all gut Gesellen am Würzburgischen Hof grüßen, auch Herrn von Grumbach." (On Wilhelm von Grumbach ["Reichstritter"] see NDB, vol. 7, pp. 212-13.) At the end of his letter Hutten writes: "Grüsse mir alle unsere Nachbaren und Freund, insonderheit Balthasar Rabensteinern und Jorg von Libra (Bibra?), Wilhelm von Hessberg und alle gute Gesellen, Sagt auch Herrn N. von Thüngen meines gnl. Herrn Bruder mein Dienst." (N. von Thüngen is undoubtedly Konrad III von Thüngen, Bishop of Würzburg [†1540]. See ADB, vol. 16, pp. 632-34). "Zeitung aus India," p. 93. Grumbach, Rabenstein, Bibra, and Hessberg, were prominent Würzburg families. Cf. A. Amrhein, "Reihenfolge der Mitglieder des adligen Domstiftes zu Würzburg," *Archiv des historischen Vereins von Unterfranken und Aschaffenburg*, 33 (1890), pp. 22, 228, 284, etc. Georg v. Bibra died as a canon of the Würzburg Cathedral in 1536.

⁵¹ Ep. V, pp. 144-5. Cf. footnote no 31.

⁵² We suspect that Faustus was a frequent guest in the home of Stibar, which Camerarius himself often visited. "...als (Stibar) 1532 durch Kauf in den Besitz des Hofes Osternach, einer Domherrenkurie, gelangt, mag dieses Haus dank seiner großzügigen Gastfreundschaft ein Mittelpunkt des geistigen Lebens der Stadt geworden sein." Mayer, p. 489.

⁵³ "Nos Caroli celebratiunculas emisimus cupidissime, itaque minus elaboratas, sed probari cupio voluntatem. Tibi dedicavimus, et fecimus Philippi Huteni mentionem temere quidem ut video, sed honorifice tamen, quare gratum fratri illius me fecisse confido." Joachim Camerarius, *Libellus novus* (Leipzig: H. Rambau, 1568), fol. Xᵛ. Cf. footnote no. 27.

⁵⁴ "Prid. Non. noctem moestissimam sustinui cum Luna Marti objiceretur in Piscibus. Faustus enim tuus facit, ut tecum lubeat ista disserere, qui utinam docueris te potius aliquid ex hac arte, quam inflaverit ventulo vanissimae superstitionis, aut nescio quibus praestigiis suspensum tenuerit. Sed quid ille ait nobis tandem? Quid etiam? Scio enim te diligenter de omnibus percontatum. Caesar ne vincit? Ita quidem fieri necesse est." *Libellus novus*, fol. X.

⁵⁵ Ptolemy, *Tetrabiblos*, I, 5 and 13; III, 12.

⁵⁶ Zinner, p. 79.

⁵⁷ Warburg, p. 498.

⁵⁸ "De bello Gallico iam fama omnes suspensos tenet. Quod sine maxima & insperata mutatione rerum vix abiturum esse credendum. Sed hoc μαντικῇ μὲν οὐ λέγω, τοῖς πράγμασιν δέ ut ait Tiresias apud Euripidem: ne tu me tanquam astrologum, quod soles, irrideas." Ep. VI, p. 394. Cf. Euripides, *The Bachanals*, 1. 368-69.

⁵⁹ Ep. V, p. 146. *Libellus novus*, fol. Xᵛ.

⁶⁰ Karl Halm, "Über die handschriftliche Sammlung der Camerarii und ihre Schicksale," *Sitzungsberichte der philosophisch-philologischen und historischen Klasse der K.b. Akademie der Wissenschaften*, 3 (1873), 247.

⁶¹ CR III, cols. 165-66.

⁶² Allen, vol. 10, p. 341.

⁶³ CR III, cols. 105-06. Warburg, p. 500.

⁶⁴ CR X, cols. 712-15; 715-17; CR XX, cols. 261-66.

⁶⁵ Cf. footnote number 34.

⁶⁶ CR III, col. 164.

⁶⁷ CR III, cols. 419-21.

⁶⁸ CR XXIV, col. 455 and CR XXV, col. 697. Also in Palmer and More, pp. 99-100.

⁶⁹ For the Latin text see chapter V, n. 10. The reliability of Manlius was questioned by many contemporaries, including Caspar Peucer and Joachim Camerarius. Beutler, pp. 188-89. H. H. Düntzer, "Die Sage von Doctor Johannes Faust," in J. Scheible, *Das Kloster* (Stuttgart, 1847), vol. 5, p. 46. Cf. chapter I, n. 3.

⁷⁰ Ep. VI, p. 197.
⁷¹ "De bello & ominationes et sermones hominum diversi sunt. Nostra oratio exijt, vel potius praecipitata fuit: quam recudemus, si recte fieri poterit." Ep. VI, p. 211.
⁷² Letter to Christoph Carlowitz: "...Etsi, u verum fatear, huic generi indies minus tribuere incipio multis de caussis, quas referre esset & longum & alienum. Quod autem ad illam totam attinet, quia hac tempora incidunt in articulum mutationis fatalis, sit vt coniectura de singularibus euentis admodu sint incertae... (Conversiones) enim magnae tanquam procellae quaedam ventorum minores alias corripere et pervertere consueuerunt. Hoc loco quae mihi in mentem veniunt, & quae te de hac mentione requirere animo tuo suspicor, ea litteris committenda non putaui. Reseruentur igitur sermonibus nostris... Prognostica Gallica studiose perquisita non reperiuntur. Vale." Ep. VI, pp. 64-65.
⁷³ Ep. VI, p. 223.
⁷⁴ Lynn Thorndike, *A History of Magic and Experimental Science* (New York, 1941), V, p. 11.

Notes – IV. The Death of Faustus

¹ "Das aber die pratik solcher kunst nit allain gottlos, sondern zum höchsten sorgclich, das ist unlaugenbar, dann sich das in der erfarnus beweist, und wissen, wie es dem weitberüempten schwarzkunstler, dem Fausto ergangen. Derselbig ist nach vilen wunderbarlichen sachen, die er bei seinem leben gelebt, darvon auch ain besonderer tractat wer zu machen, letztlich in der herrschaft Staufen im Preisgew in großen alter vom bösen gaist umgebracht worden... Es ist auch umb die zeit (i.e. ca. 1541) der Faustus zu oder nit weit von Staufen, dem Stetlin Breisgew, gestorben. Der ist bei seiner zeit ein wunderbarlicher nigromanta gewest, als er bei unsern zeiten hat mögen in deutschen landen erfunden werden, der auch so vil seltzamer hendel gehapt hin und wider, das sein in vil jaren nit leuchtlichen wurt vergessen werden. Ist ain alter mann worden und, wie man sagt, elengclichen gestorben. Vil haben allerhandt anzeigungen und vermuetungen noch vermaint, der bös gaist, den er in seinen lebzeiten nur sein schwager genannt, hab ine umbracht. Die buecher, die er verlasen, sein dem herren von Staufen, in dessen herrschaft er abgangen, zu handen worden, darumb doch hernach vil leut haben geworben und daran meins erachtens ein sorgclichen und ungluckhaftigen schatz und gabe begert. Den munchen zu Luxhaim im Wassichin hat er ain gespenst in das closter verbannet, desen sie in vil jaren nit haben künden abkommen und sie wunderbarlich hat molestiert, allain der ursach, das sie ine einsmals nit haben wellen übernacht behalten, darumb hat er inen den unrüebigen gast geschafft." Palmer and More, pp. 103-5.
² "Daß die Zimmersche Familiengeschichte gelegentlich hochinteressant und sehr wertvoll ist, daneben aber ebenso schwankhaft, skandalsüchtig und redselig und deshalb unzuverlässig sein kann: darin sind sich die Verfasser all dieser Einzeluntersuchungen einig." Beat Rudolf Jenny, *Graf Froben Christoph von Zimmern. Geschichtsschreiber. Erzähler. Landesherr. Ein Beitrag zur Geschichte des Humanismus in Schwaben* (Lindau: J. Thorbecke, 1959), p. 24.
³ According to the equally unreliable report of Manlius, Faustus died in Württemberg. Cf. Henning, pp. 111-2 and 132.
⁴ Karl Sudhoff, "Philipp Begardi und sein *Index sanitatis*. Ein Beitrag zur Geschichte des Ärztestandes und des Kurpfuschertums in der ersten Hälfte des 16. Jahrhunderts," *Archiv für die Geschichte der Medizin*, 1 (1908), pp. 103-4.
⁵ "Von den bösen vngeschaffenen, vntüglichen, trughaftigen, vnnützen, vnd auch vngelarten ärtzten etc. und auch, wo bei man sie erkennen mag." Philipp Begardi, *Index sanitatis. Ein schöns*

vnd vast nützliches Büchlin / genant Zeyger der gesundtheyt / den jhnen / so kranck seind / vnd nit wissens haben / wie / wo vnd was massen sie widerumb bekommen mögen vnd erlangen recht volkommende gesundtheyt zu trost gemacht vnd an tag geben (Worms: S. Wagner, 1539).

6 "Wil hie nun aber dise sach faren lassen / vnd fürther gehn zu eyner andern gattung / auch diser gesellschafft. Es wirt noch eyn namhafftiger dapfferer mann erfunden: ich wolt aber doch seinen namen nit genent haben / so wil er auch nit verborgen sein / noch vnbekant. Dann er ist vor etlichen jaren vast durch alle landschafft / Fürstenthuomb vnnd Königreich gezogen / seinen namen jederman selbs bekant gemacht / vnd seine große kunst / nit alleyn der artznei / sonder auch Chirmancei / Nigramancei / Visionomei / Visiones imm Cristal / vnd dergleichen mer künst / sich höchlich berümpt. Vnd auch nit alleyn berümpt, sonder sich auch eynen berümpten vnd erfarnen meyster bekant vnnd geschriben. Hat auch selbs bekant / vnd nit geleugknet / daß er sei / vnnd heyß Faustus, domit sich geschriben Philosophum Philosophorum etc. Wie vil aber mir geklagt haben, daß sie von jm betrogen worden, deren ist eyn grosse zal gewesen. Nun sein verheyssen ware auch groß / wie des Tessali: dergleichen sein rhüm / wie auch des Theophrasti: aber die that / wie ich noch vernimm, vast kleyn vnd betrüglich erfunden: doch hat er sich im gelt nemen, oder empfahen (das ich auch recht red) nit gesaumpt / vnd nachmals auch im abzugk / er hat / wie ich beracht / vil mit den ferßen gesegnet. Aber was soll man nun darzu thun, hin ist hin / ich wil es jetzt auch do bei lassen / lug du weiter / was du zuschicken hast." Begardi, p. XVII. Cf. Palmer and More, pp. 94-5 and Meyer, p. 337.

Notes – V. Luther and the New Image of Faustus

1 "De Fausto Necromantico. – Diuertitur sub noctem coenobium quoddam, valde diues, pernoctaturus illic. Fraterculus apponit illi uile uinum, pendulum, ac nihil gratiae habens, rogat Faustus ut ex uase alter hauriat melius uinum, quod nobilibus dare consueuerat. Fraterculus mox dixit, Clauses non habeo, prior dormit, quem exuscitare piaculum est. Faustus inquit, Claues iacent isto angulo, has accipe, & uas illud ad sinistrum latus aperi, & adfer mihi potum. Fraterculus renuit, sibi non esse commissum à Priori aliud uninum hospitibus proponere. Faustus ijs auditis, iratus dixit, Videbis breui momento mira inhospitalis fratercule. Abijt summo mane insalutato hospite, ira accensus, ac immisit satanam quendam furibundum, die noctuque in coenobio perstrepentem, omnia mouentem tam in ecclesia, quam in ipsi habitationibus monarchorum, adeo ut quietem nullam habere possint, quodcumque negotium attentarent. Tandem deliberarunt, an coenubium esset reliquendum, aut omnino pereundum. Palatino itaque scripserunt de infortunio illo, quo tenebantur. Qui coenobium in suam recepit defensionem, abiectis monachis, quibus alimenta praestat in singulos annos, reliqua sibi seruat. Aiunt quidam, etsi adhuc hodie monachi coenobium intrent, tantas turbationes fieri, ut quitem incolentes habere non possint. Hoc nouit satan instituere. – Aliud de Fausto exemplum. – Basileae cum illo coenatus sum in collegio magno, qui uarij generis aues, nescio ubi emerat, aut quis dederat, cum hoc temporis nullae uenderentur, coquo ad assandum praebuerat. Quales etiam ego nunquam in nostris regionibus uiderim. Canem secum ducebat & equum, Satanas fuisse reor, qui ad omnia erant parati exequenda. Canem aliquando serui formam assumere, & esculenta adferre, quidam mihi dixere. Atqui miser deplorandum finem sortius est, nam a satana suffocatus, cuius cadauer in feretro facie ad terram perpetuo spectans, etsi quinquies in tergum uerteretur. Dominus custodiat nos, ne satanae mancipia fiamus." Johannes Gast, *Tomus secundus convivalium sermonum* (Basel: N. Brylinger, 1548), pp. 280-1. For the English text see Palmer and More, pp. 97-8.

2 Paul Burckhardt writes: "Gewisse Stücke der Sermonen, die aus dem Tagebuch stammen, hat Gast für Buchausgabe zu epischer Breite erweitert und rhetorisch stilisiert." Paul Burckhardt, "Die schriftstellerische Tätigkeit des Johannes Gast," *Basler Zeitschrift für Geschichte und Altertumskunde*, 42 (1943), 185. Cf. Paul Burckhardt, *Das Tagebuch des Johannes Gast* (Basel: Schwabe, 1945), p. 16.

3 Burckhardt, "Die schriftstellerische Tätigkeit," pp. 176-8; & Burckhardt, *Das Tagebuch*, pp. 50 & 94.

4 Burckhardt, "Die schriftstellerische Tätigkeit," pp. 188-9.

5 See table conversation nos. 5358b and 6830. All references to Luther's conversations are from Martin Luther, *Tischreden* (Weimar: Böhlau, 1912-21). Cf. Barbara Allen Woods, *The Devil in Dog Form. A Partial Type Index of Devil Legends*, in *Folklore Studies*, no. 11 (Berkeley: Univ. of Calif. Press, 1959).

6 *Tischreden*, nos. 6809 & 6815; Erich Klinger, *Luther und der deutsche Volksaberglaube*, in *Palaestra* 56 (1912), p. 33. The author of the preface to the 1587 Volksbuch thought in similar terms: "In summa, der Teuffel lohnet seinen Dienern, wie der Hencker seinem Knecht, unnd nemmen die Teuffelsbeschwerer selten ein gut Ende, wie auch an D. Johann Fausto zusehen, der noch bey Menschen Gedächtnis gelebet, seine Verschreibung unnd Bündnis mit dem Teufel gehabt, viel setzsamer Abenthewr und grewliche Schandt und Laster getrieben, mit fressen, sauffen, Hurerey und aller Uppigkeit, bis im zu letzt der Teuffel seinen verdienten Lohn gegeben, und jm den Hals erschrecklicher weis umgedreht." Hans Henning (ed.), *Historia von D. Johannes Fausten* (Halle: Sprache u. Literatur, 1963), p. 9. Cf. Milschack, Col. 270.

7 Burckhardt, *Das Tagebuch*, pp. 93-4.

8 See chapter I, footnote no. 3.

9 Hans Henning, *Faust-Bibliographie*, pp. 82-3, and Alexander Tille, *Die Faustsplitter in der Literatur des sechzehnten bis achtzehnten Jahrhunderts nach den ältesten Quellen* (Berlin: Felber, 1900), pp. 17-21.

10 "Noui quendam nomine Faustum de Kundling, quod est paruum oppidum, patriae meae uicinum. Hic cum esset scholasticus Cracouiensis, ibi magiam didicerat, sicut ibi olim fuit eius magnus usus, & ibidem fuerunt publicae eiusdem artis professiones. Vagabutur passim, dicebat arcana multa. Ille Venetijs cum uellet ostendere spectaculum, dixit se uolaturum in coelum. Diabolus igitur subuexit eum, & afflixit adeò, ut allisus hume penè exanimatus esset: sed tamen non est mortuus.

Ante paucos annos idem Ioannes Faustus, postremo die sedit admodum moestus in quodam pago ducatus Vuirtenbergensis. Hospes ipsum alloquitur, cur moestus esset praeter morem & consuetudinem (erat alioqui turpissimus nebulo, inquinatissimae uitae, ita ut semel atque iterum penè interfectus sit propter libidines) ibi dixit hospiti in illo pago: Ne perterrefias hac nocte. Media nocte domus quassata est. Mane cum Faustus non surgeret, & iam esset fere meridies, hospes adhibitis alijs, ingressus est in eius conclaue, inuentique cum iacentem prope lectum inuersa facie, à diabolo interfectus. Viuens, adhuc habebat secum canem, qui erat diabolus, sicut iste nebulo qui scripsit De uanitate artium etiam habebat canem, secum curentem, qui erat diabolus. Hic Faustus in hoc oppido Vuittemberga euasit, cum optimus princeps dux Ioannes dedisset mandata de illo capiendo, sic Norimbergae etiam euasit, cum iam inciperet prandere, aestuauit, surgitque statim, soluens quod hospiti debebat, uix autem uenerat ante portam, ubi ueniunt lictores, & de eo inquirunt.

Idem Faustus magus, turpissima bestia, & cloaca multorum diabolorum, uanè floriabatur de se omnes uictorias, quas habuerunt Caesarini exercitus in Italia, esse partas per ipsum sua magia. Idque fuit mendacium uanissimum. Id enim dico propter iuuentutem, ne statim talibus uanis hominibus assentiantur." *Locorum communium collectanea* (Basel: J. Oporinus, 1562), pp. 42-4. For the English text see Palmer and More, pp. 101-3.

Notes – V. Luther and the New Image of Faustus

11 Palmer and More, p. 99. Cf. Milschack, Col. 234!
12 Ibid., pp. 99-100.
13 "Cum forte in coena facta fuisset mentio magi cuisdam nomine Fausti, dixit Doctor serio: Diabolus non utitur opera magorum contra me, sed si potuisset me laedere, iam diu fecisset. Er hat mich wol beim kopff schon gehabt und hat mich dennoch mussen ghen lassen. O, ich hab in wol versucht, das ich nicht hab gewust, ob ich tod oder lebendig bin, hat mich auch in verzweifelung bracht, das ich nicht wuste, ob ein Gott were, und an unserm Herrn Gott gar versagt. Summa, da ist kein hilff noch radt denn Gott selbs immediate; der kan einem darnach mit eim einigen wortlin helffen..." Aurifaber adds a title to his text, which is slightly different, is: "Gottes wort allein uberwindet des Teufels feurige Pfeile und alle Anfechtungen. – Da uber Tisch zu Abends eines Schwarzkünstlers, Faustus genannt, gedacht ward, saget Doctor Martinus ernstlich: "Der Teufel gebraucht der Zäuberer Dienst wider mich nicht; hätte er mir gekonnt und vermocht Schaden zu thun, er hätte es lange gethan. Er hat mich wol oftmals schon bei dem Kopf gehabt, aber er hat mich dennoch mussen gehen lassen. Ich hab ihn wol versucht, was er fur ein Geist ist. Er hat mir oft so hart zugesetzt, daß ich nicht gewußt hàb, ob ich todt oder lebendig sei. Er hat mich auch wol in Verzweifelung gebracht, daß ich nicht wußte, ob auch ein Gott wäre und an unserm lieben Herrn Gott ganz und gar verzagte. Aber mit Gottes Wort hab ich mich seiner erwehret. Es ist sonst auch keine Hülfe noch Rath, denn daß Gott (mit einem Wörtlin durch Menschen gesprochen, oder das einer sonst ergreift) einem hilft. Hat man aber Gottes Wort nicht, so ists balde um uns geschehen, denn da kann er die Leute nach seinem Willen reiten und treiben." *Tischreden*, no. 1059.
14 "De ludificatoribus et arte magica fiebat mentio, quomodo Sathan homines excaecaret. Multa dicebant de Fausto, welcher den Teufel seynen schwoger hies, und hat sich lassen horen, wen ich, Martin Lutter, ihm nur di handt gereycht hette, wolt er mich vorterbet haben; aber ich wolde in nicht geschawet haben, porrexissem illi manus in nomine Domini Deo protectore. Nam credo in me multa veneficia contra me structa esse." *Tischreden*, no. 3601. For the English text see Palmer and More, p. 93.
15 *Tischreden*, no. 2982.
16 Ibid., no. 2370.
17 Otto Scheel, *Martin Luther. Vom Katholizismus zur Reformation* (Tübingen: Mohr, 1930), p. 110.
18 Martin Luther, *Werke* (Weimar: Böhlau, 1914), vol. 40:2, pp. 112-3.
19 Martin Luther, *Werke* (Weimar: Böhlau, 1911), vol. 40:1, p. 315.
20 Klingner, p. 87.
21 *Tischreden*, nos. 3841, 6836, etc. & Klingner, pp. 64-91.
22 *Tischreden*, nos. 1425, 5479, and 4450.
23 "Daher gehoeren auch, die es gar zu grob treiben und mit dem Teuffel ein bund machen, das er yhn gelt gnug gebe odder zur bulschafft helffe, yhr viech beware, verloren gut widderschaffe etc. Als die zeuberer und schwartzkünstige." *(Werke*, vol. 30:1, p. 134) Quoted from Klingner, p. 31; cf. pp. 30-2, 35, 45, & 134.
24 "Von einem Wahrsager. – Zu E. ward ein Wahrsager und Schwarzkunstiger verbrannt, der etliche Jahr traurig und betrübt war gangen darum, daß er sehr arm war und hatte weder zu beissen noch zu brocken. Da begegnete ihm ein Mal der Teufel in einer sichtlichen Gestalt und verhiess ihm Großes, daß er sollte reich werden, wenn er die Taufe und die Erlösung, durch Christum geschehen, verleugnen und nimmermehr Busse thun wollte. Der Arme nahm solchs an; da gab ihm der Teufel von Stund an ein Krystall, darauss er konnte wahrsagen, dadurch bekam er einen großen Namen und ein groß Zulaufen, daß er reich drüber ward. Endlich betrog ihn der Teufel redlich und ließ ihn in Hintern sehen, daß er etliche unschüldige Leute aus der Krystallen angab und Dieberei bezüchtigte. Dadurch verursachte er, daß er ward ins Gefängnis gelegt, und

bekannte darnach, daß er den Bund, mit dem Teufel gemacht, gebrochen hätte, bat, man wollte einen Prediger lassen zu ihm gehen. Thät rechtschaffene Busse und brachte mit seinem Exempel viel Leute zu Gottesfurcht, und starb mit fröhlichem Herzen in seiner Leibesstrafe. Also hat sich der Teufel in seiner eigenen Kunst beschmissen und in seinen bösen Anschlägen und Tücken offenbaret." *Tischreden*, no. 3618B.

24 Klingner, p. 32.
25 Goethe's conversation with Heinrich Voss on February 24, 1805. J. W. Goethe, *Gedenkausgabe der Werke, Briefe, und Gespräche*, XXII, (Zürich, Artemis, 1949), 365.
26 Cf. Barbara Könneker, "Deutsche Literatur im Zeitalter des Humanismus und der Reformation," *Neues Handbuch der Literaturwissenschaft*, ed. Klaus von See, IX, (Frankfurt: Athenaion, 1974), 166. For further information on this general topic see Erich Schmidt, "Faust und Luther," *Sitzungsberichte der königlichen Preußischen Akademie der Wissenschaften zu Berlin, Phil.-hist. Klasse*, 25 (1896), 567-91, and Eugen Wolff, *Luther und Faust* (Halle: Niemeyer, 1912). Keith L. Roos, *The Devil in 16th Century Literature: The Teufelsbücher* (Bern & Frankfurt: Lang, 1972), pp. 24-5.

Notes – VI. The Metamorphosis of Faustus

1 Erich Kahler, *The Orbit of Thomas Mann* (Princeton: Princeton Univ. Press, 1969), p. 97. Cf. Ernest Cushing Richardson "Faust and the Clementine Recognitions," *Papers of the American Society of Church History* 6 (1894), 133-45.
2 Georg Lukács writes: "... Gorki hat durchaus recht, wenn er meint, daß solche Sagen wie die vom Faust *nicht 'Früchte der Phantasie' sind, sondern vollkommen gesetzmäßige und notwendige Übertreibungen der realen Fakten. Es sind große reale historische Lebenstendenzen, welche die dichterische Arbeit des Volkes auf das Wesen gebracht und auf diesem Niveau zu Gestalten verdichtet hat.*" Georg Lukács, *Goethe und seine Zeit* (Berlin: Aufbau, 1950, p. 203.
3 Wolfgang Kayser, *Die Wahrheit der Dichter* (Hamburg: Rowohlt, 1959), p. 11.
4 About this intolerant climate cf. Norman Cohn, *Europe's Inners Demons. An Enquiry Inspired by the Great Witch-Hunt* (London: Sussex University Press, 1975) H. C. Erik Midelfort, *Witch Hunting in Southwestern Germany. 1562-1684. The Social and Intellectual Foundations* (Stanford: Univ. Press, 1972). For general orientation see also E. William Monter, "The Historiography of European Witchcraft: Progress and Prospects," *Journal of Interdisciplinary History* 2 (1972), 435-51; Jeffrey Burton Russell, *Witchcraft in the Middle Ages* (Ithaca: Cornell University Press, 1972); Keith Thomas, *Religion and the Decline of Magic* (London: Weidenfeld and Nicolson, 1971).
5 This was the age of the prominent French philosopher and statesman Jean Bodin (1530-96), who, like Luther, was an opponent of Renaissance magic as well as witchcraft. In a recent article Frances Yates has suggested that this attitude may be symptomatic of a fundamental change. Bodin "may represent something like a crisis in the European tradition, a shift from Renaissance occultism... Is it possible that the European witch craze might be, in one of its aspect, a symptom of this shift?" Frances Yates, "The Mystery of Jean Bodin," *The New York Review of Books*, 23 (1976), 48.
6 H. R. Trevor-Roper, "The European Witch-craze of the Sixteenth and Seventeenth Centuries," in: *Religion, the Reformation and Social Change* (London: Macmillan, 1972), pp. 136-7. "The recrudescence of the witch-craze from about 1560 can be documented from innumerable sources" Ibid., p. 140. "The responsibility of the Protestant clergy for the revival of the witch-

craze in the mid-sixteenth century is undeniable." Ibid., p. 138. Cf. Ibid., p. 141. Cf. W. G. Soldan & H. Heppe, *Geschichte der Hexenprozesse*, newly edited by M. Bauer (München: M. Müller, 1912), pp. 421 ff.

7 For example, in 1589 in the town of Quedlinburg (Saxony) 133 witches *are said* to have been burned; between 1587 and 1593 in villages around Trier more than 1000 persons were accused of being witches, and of these 368 were burned. For these as well as other figures on persecution of witches see H. C. Lea, *Materials Toward a History of Witchcraft*, arranged and edited by. A. C. Howland (Philadelphia: University of Pennsylvanlia Press, 1939), III, 1075-1142.

INDEX

Aesop 53
Agricola, Rudolph 18, 19, 20
Agrippa von Nettesheim, Heinrich Cornelius 74-75, 87
Albert the Great 24
Albrecht (Duke of Prussia) 53
Andrelinus, Publius Faustus 32
Apel, Johannes 53
Aquinas, Thomas 19, 46
Aristotle 18, 22, 29, 35
Augustine 32
Aurifaber, Johannes 78

Begardi, Philipp 68
Beheim, Lorenz 43
Bonaventura 46
Bostius, Arnold 24, 25
von Brandenburg, Joachim 25, 31
Buitzius, Conrad 21
von Burkhard, Ulrich 43

Camerarius, Joachim 13, 22, 48-66, 76, 85, 87
Capellarius, Johannes 28
Carion, Johannes 54
Celtis, Conrad 15, 19, 20, 33
Charles V (Emperor) 56-59, 61-62, 64, 65
Cicero 53
Copernicus, Nicolaus 51, 54
Cusanus, Nicolaus 15
Cremona, Gerhart of 20

von Dalberg, Johannes 19-21
Dürer, Albrecht 43-44

Eberbach, Peter 41
Eichmann, Jodocus 21
Ellinger, Georg 48-49
Erasmus, Desiderius 33, 44, 55-56, 62
Ezra 29, 34

Ficino 20, 26
Francis I 64
Fredrick III (Emperor) 80
Fuchs, Andreas 43
Fuchs, Jacob 43

Gaguin, Robert 33
Galen 53
Gallus, Libanius 27
de Ganay, Germanus 25, 27-28, 33
Gast, Johannes 70-76, 81
Gaurico, Luca 65
Georg Schenk von Limburg 42-44, 85
Goethe, Johann Wolfgang
von Grimmelshausen, H.J.C. 83

Hasse, Johannes 17
Henning, Hans 9, 11, 14
Hering, Loy 43-44
Hephaestion of Thebes 52
Hermes Trismegistus 20, 25-26, 30, 40, 52
Hesse, Eobanus 55, 61, 62
Hoest, Stephan 19
Holzschuher, Hieronymus 13, 51
Homer 56, 58
von Hutten, Moritz 54-59, 62
von Hutten, Philipp 13, 44, 54-60, 64, 85
von Hutten, Ulrich 43, 55

von Inghen, Marsilius 19
Ireneus 34
Isidor 32

Laetus, Pomponio 32
Lauterbach, Antonius 78-79
Leib, Kilian 13, 45-48, 85
Lessing 13, 15
Lubler, Syrus 17
Luder, Peter 19
Luther, Martin 8, 12, 14, 47, 53, 65, 68, 70-82, 86

Macrobius   53
Manlius, Johannes   12, 15, 63, 64, 73-77, 81, 83-84
Marlowe, Christopher   83
Maximilian (Emperor)   33
Medler, Nicolaus   78
Melanchthon, Philipp   8, 9, 12, 30, 47, 50-76, 81
Moses   34
Müller, Johannes   13, 44
Müller (Regiomontanus), Johannes   50-51
Müller, Johannes (Cf. *Zimmerische Chronik*)   67
Mutinaus Rufus, Conrad   13, 15, 31, 35, 39, 42, 44, 55, 69, 85

von Nassau, Heinrich   56
Nebuchadnezzar   34
Nero   68, 75

Ockham, William of   19

Paracelsus, Theophrastus   51, 68
Perlach, Andreas   52
Peuckert, Will-Erich   11
Peuerbach, Georg   52
Pfefferkorn, Johannes   40
Pfinzing, Melchior
Philipp of the Palatinate (Elector)   28, 30, 36
Pico della Mirandola, Giovanni   20, 23, 26-27, 38, 40, 46
Pirckheimer, Willibald   43, 45
Plato   26, 29, 35
von Pleningen   19, 21
Pliny the Younger   19
Poliander, Johannes   54
Pompilius, Numa   32
Ptolemy   52, 54

Quintilian   53

Reuchlin, Johannes   19, 20, 26, 36, 40-41

Richard of Middletown   46
Rubeanus, Crotus   43, 55

Sabellicus, Marcus Antonius   32-33
de Sacrobosco, Johannes   20
Schedel, Hartmann   18
Schliemann, Heinrich   9, 83
Schöner, Johannes   43, 44, 50-53, 61
Schottenloher, Karl   47
von Schwarzenberg, Johannes   43
von Sickingen, Franz   29, 36-37, 42, 44, 85
Simon Magus   75, 86
Sophocles   53
Spalatin, Georg   36
Spengler, Lazarus   44
Stibar, Daniel   42, 44, 53-63, 85
Stöffler, Johannes   46, 52, 54

Theocritus   53
Theon of Alexandria   52
Theophilus   81
Thessalus   68
Trenchard, John   32
Trithemius, Jacob   28
Trithemius, Johannes   13, 19-20, 22, 23-39, 40-41, 44-45, 49-50, 61, 79-80, 83, 85

Urban, Heinrich   39

Valens, Vettius   52
Virdung von Haßfurt, Johannes   23, 28, 30-31, 36-38, 76
Virgil   58

Werner, Johannes   50
von Westerburg, Johannes   25
Wimpfeling, Jacob   19
Witkowski, Georg   17
Wolf, Hans   43-44

von Zimmern, Froben Christoph   67
Zoroaster   32, 86

Humanistische Bibliothek

Reihe I: Abhandlungen
(Bitte auch den Sonderprospekt anfordern –
enthält: Reihe II: Texte, Reihe III: Skripten.)

1. Eckhard Keßler
Das Problem des frühen Humanismus
Seine philosophische Bedeutung bei Coluccio
Salutati
227 S. kart. DM 48,–

2. Eike Barmeyer
Die Musen
Ein Beitrag zur Inspirationstheorie
228 S. kart. DM 48,–

3. Werner Raith
Die Macht des Bildes
Ein humanistisches Problem bei Gianfrancesco Pico della Mirandola
110 S. kart. DM 28,–

4. Klaus-Peter Lange
Theoretiker des literarischen Manierismus
Tesauros und Pellegrinis Lehre von der
"acutezza" oder von der Macht der Sprache
176 S. kart. DM 38,–

5. Peter Crome
Symbol und Unzulänglichkeit der Sprache
Jamblichos, Plotin, Porphyrios, Proklos
222 S. kart. DM 58,–

6. Richard Blank
Sprache und Dramaturgie
Die aischyleische Kassandraszene – das
Osterspiel von Klosterneuburg – Machiavellis
"Mandragola"
235 S. kart. DM 48,–

7. Jochen Schlobach
Zyklentheorie und Epochenmetaphorik
Studien zur bildlichen Sprache der Geschichtsreflexion in Frankreich von der Renaissance
bis zur Frühaufklärung
Ca. 380 S. kart. ca. DM 84,–

8. Hella Theill-Wunder
Die archaische Verborgenheit
Die philosophischen Wurzeln der negativen
Theologie
204 S. kart. DM 58,–

9. Konrad Krautter
Philologische Methode und humanistische Existenz
Filippo Beroaldo und sein Kommentar zum
Goldenen Esel des Apuleius
224 S. kart. DM 58,–

10. Janos Riesz
Die Sestine
Ihre Stellung in der literarischen Kritik und
ihre Geschichte als lyrisches Genus
328 S. kart. DM 78,–

11. Dietrich Harth
Philologie und praktische Philosophie
Untersuchungen zum Sprach- und Traditionsverständnis des Erasmus von Rotterdam
192 S. kart. DM 40,–

12. Werner Schmidt
Theorie der Induktion
Die prinzipielle Bedeutung der Epagoge bei
Aristoteles
239 S. kart. DM 48,–

13. Hanna-Barbara Gerl
Rhetorik als Philosophie
Lorenzo Valla
296 S. kart. DM 78,–

14. Günther List
Chiliastische Utopie und radikale Reformation
Die Erneuerung der Idee vom Tausendjährigen Reich im 16. Jahrhundert
269 S. kart. DM 68,–

15. Matthias Wesseler
Die Einheit von Wort und Sache
Der Entwurf einer rhetorischen Philosophie
bei Marius Nizolius
202 S. kart. DM 48,–

16. Eginhard Hora / Eckhard Keßler, Hrsg.
Studia Humanitatis
Ernesto Grassi zum 70. Geburtstag
344 S. und Frontispiz sowie 1 Kunstdrucktafel, Ln. DM 78,–

17. Joachim Dalfen
Polis und Poiesis
Die Auseinandersetzung bei Platon und seinen Zeitgenossen
335 S. kart. DM 98,–

18. Barbara Tiemann
Fabel und Emblem
Die Bedeutung Gilles Corrozets für die französische Fabeldichtung der Renaissance
272 S. und 40 Abb. auf Kunstdruck
kart. DM 80,–

19. Jack V. Haney
From Italy to Muscovy
The Life and Works of Maxim the Greek
198 S. kart. DM 58,–

20. Josef IJsewijn / Eckhard Keßler, Hrsg.
Acta Conventus Neo-Latini Lovaniensis
Proceedings of the First International Congress of Neo-Latin Studies at Louvain
769 S. Ln. DM 320,–

21. Paul Oskar Kristeller
Humanismus und Renaissance I
Die antiken und mittelalterlichen Quellen. Aus dem Englischen übersetzt von Renate Schweyen-Ott, hrsg. von Eckhard Keßler
259 S. Ln. DM 78,–

22. Paul Oskar Kristeller
Humanismus und Renaissance II
Philosophie, Bildung und Kunst. Aus dem Englischen übersetzt von Renate Schweyen-Ott, hrsg. von Eckhard Keßler
346 S. Ln. DM 88,–

23. Willi Hirdt
Studien zum epischen Prolog
Der Eingang in der erzählenden Versdichtung Italiens
345 S. kart. DM 78,–

24. Joachim Camerarius (1500 – 1574)
Beiträge zur Geschichte des Humanismus im Zeitalter der Reformation / Essays on the History of Humanism during the Period of the Reformation
255 S. und 1 Frontispiz Ln. DM 68,–

25. Eckhard Keßler
Petrarca und die Geschichte
Geschichtsschreibung, Rhetorik, Philosophie im Übergang vom Mittelalter zur Neuzeit
304 S. Ln. DM 80,–

26. Pièrre Tuynman, Hrsg.
Acta Conventus Neo-Latini Amstelodamensis
Proceedings of the Second International Congress of Neo-Latin Studies at Amsterdam
ca. 1100 S. Ln. ca. DM 280,–

28. John Neubauer
Symbolismus und symbolische Logik
227 S. und 5 Kunstdrucktafeln,
kart. DM 28,–

29. Hannelore Rausch
Theoria
Von ihrer sakralen zur philosophischen Bedeutung
Ca. 256 S. kart. ca. DM 36,–

30. Josef Winniger
Die Entwicklung der Problematik in Feuerbachs Hauptwerken der dreißiger Jahre
Zur Genesis des anthropologischen Materialismus
Ca. 176 S. kart. ca. DM 36,–

31. Arnold Seifert
Logik zwischen Scholastik und Humanismus
Das Kommentarwerk Johann Ecks
183 S. kart. ca. DM 48,–

Wilhelm Fink Verlag
Nikolaistr. 2 · 8000 München 40